Hiking
the Southwest

Hiking
the Southwest

The Best Hikes in Nevada,
Arizona, Utah, and New Mexico

Branch Whitney

Huntington Press
Las Vegas, Nevada

Hiking the Southwest
The Best Hikes in Nevada, Arizona, Utah, and New Mexico

Published by
Huntington Press
3665 Procyon St.
Las Vegas, NV 89103
Phone (702) 252-0655
e-mail: books@huntingtonpress.com

ISBN: 978-1-935396-36-9

Photos: Lower Calf Creek, photo 1 ©Carl Pantuso; Dreamstime.com Images: Humphrey's Peak Panorama ©Pancaketom; Observation Point, Zion National Park, and Lower Calf Creek Falls Trail ©Andrea Hornackova; Boynton Canyon, Sedona, Arizona ©Rosswilson; Upper Yosemite Falls Trail ©Mariusz Jurgielewicz; all other photos ©Branch Whitney

Design & Production: Laurie Shaw

Dedication

This book is dedicated to Kathy.

Acknowledgments

I would like to thank the following people for their guidance and knowledge: "Crazy" Kenny Amundsen, Mark "Throw Down" Beauchamp, Davis "Dead Horse" Finley, Ed Forkos, Luba Leaf, Richard Natale, Eva Pollan, and "Wrong Way" Richard Baugh. And thanks to the gang at Huntington Press. It's great to work with people who want to do things correctly.

Contents

Introduction
to the Hikes

The book you hold in your hands contains the best hikes in the Southwest. No lame hikes here—those hikes are in the book next to this one. These are the hikes you'll be telling your grandchildren about over and over until you realize they left an hour ago. From the unbelievable turquoise water in Havasupai to the must-see phenomenon called the Wave, these are the hikes you'll want to cross off your bucket list.

For the first time in print, this book gives you crystal-clear directions to all the Southwest's favorite hikes, including detailed directions covering the backpack and hike to the Colorado River at Havasupai. No vague descriptions here. You'll never wonder if the author ever did the hike.

Are you into hardcore hikes? This book has you covered with Rim to Rim to Rim in the Grand Canyon. It's 45 miles in two days! Are you a highpointer? Then as Dwight Schrute would say, "You're an idiot!" Britton Hill in Florida, come on. However, this tome does have hikes to the highest peaks in Arizona, Nevada, and New Mexico. Like scenic hikes? Bryce Canyon is unbelievable. Want to try some canyoneering? The Subway in Zion is the perfect beginning canyoneer's adventure.

You're now (assuming you bought this book) in possession of the best hikes in the Southwest. You don't need to buy separate guidebooks for each area and you don't have to get used to different authors' writing styles. Hiking and peak bagging are the perfect activities in this economic down time. They're healthy, fun, and inexpensive. Why ever go back to work? So enjoy these hikes and remember: It's the route that makes a great hike.

How This Book Is Organized

Each of the 10 hiking destinations has a brief introduction, followed by the hikes. I don't bore you with a lot trivial and dull facts to crank up the page count (and the price). Driving directions are from the closest towns. You can obtain driving directions from where you live to the nearest town via the Internet. Each hike has information about the best season, difficulty of the hike, and other factors, so you can quickly determine if you're interested in the hike.

I don't write about the flora and fauna. Those are fancy words for plants and animals. It's not my thing and there's too much diversity. If you're interested, you can find information on the Web.

Format of the Hikes

Trailhead: Name of the trailhead and if the trailhead is marked.

Distance: Noted in miles. All distances are up and back, unless specified.

Elevation gain: How many feet you gain to the summit or destination.

Elevation of peak: Height of the peak. Listed only for hikes that go to peaks.

Time: Time it takes to complete the hike, up and back.

Difficulty: Scale 1 (easy) to 5 (very difficult).

Danger level: Scale 1 (safe) to 5 (use caution).

Class: Amount of climbing. Class 1 to Class 4. See below for more.

How easy to follow: Scale of 1 (well-maintained trail) to 5 (cross-country route).

Children: Is the hike appropriate for children (ages 5 to 11) accompanied with an adult?

Waypoints: USGS waypoints. WGS 84 datum.

Fees/Permits: If there's a fee or permit required, it's listed below with additional details.

Best season: In which season(s) to do the hike.

Driving directions: From the nearest town to the trailhead.

Permits: How to obtain official permission. Most hikes don't require permits.

Comments: Warnings, insights, and sometimes history about the hike.

Lodging: Information on where to find a motel room and campsite reservations.

The hike: Step-by-step guide to the hike.

Trails Versus Routes

The hikes in this book are classified as either trails or routes. Some hikes follow trails, then become routes once they leave the trail. There's a huge difference between trails and routes. A trail hike is very easy to follow and generally well-marked. To return, just retrace your steps on the same trail.

A route is much harder to follow. I have photos of key landmarks to look for and waypoints you can enter into your GPS unit. I realize not everyone has or uses a GPS. All of the hikes can be followed without a GPS, though using a GPS is very helpful. But it all comes down to common sense. People were doing these hikes long before anyone heard of a GPS or waypoints. You should never rely solely on a GPS unit. If it quits working, well, you're SOL.

An example of a trail hike is Angels Landing in Zion National Park. You'd have to work at getting lost. It's well-maintained and clearly marked. The hike to Black Velvet Peak in Red Rock Canyon is a route. Once you leave the trail, you navigate by landmarks. These types of hikes are much harder to follow and should only be attempted by experienced hikers. It's unlikely you'll see another hiker on a route.

Time Estimates

Time estimates are averages. Some hikers will finish the hike much sooner; others will take much longer. The rest of you will make me look like I'm psychic. Once you do a few hikes, you'll have a better idea of how my time estimates apply to you.

Dangers

Due to rock fall, some of the hikes in this book are dangerous. If hiking in a group, be very careful not to dislodge rocks. Test your handholds before committing to a move.

To minimize the danger, always hike in a group (four hikers are the best), tell someone where you're hiking and when you believe you'll be back. Cell-phone coverage is still spotty (boy, that's a surprise!), but you can always try to make a call.

Tip: Turn your phone off until you need it. Your battery will last a lot longer when it's not constantly searching for a signal.

Class Grades

Class 1—Like walking on a sidewalk.

Class 2—Hiking over uneven terrain. Hands are used for balance only.

Class 3—Climbing requires using hands and feet. Exposure is minimal.

Class 4—Climbing steep rock. Exposure can be significant. A rope is recommended.

Class 5—Technical rock climbing. Does not apply to hikes in this book.

Weather

Weather is a major concern. Hike the Subway during a flash flood and you'll no longer have to worry about taxes! This is pretty simple: Check the Internet before you hike. If not, you could be sweating in 110+ temperatures or freezing in below-zero temperatures. Come prepared for cold weather if hiking at high elevation. When you're higher than 12,000 feet, it can snow even during summer months.

The rule of thumb is weather forecasts aren't dependable more than three days out. There are several good websites for weather. I like www.wrh.noaa.gov/. You can pinpoint the elevation you will be hiking or camping at by clicking on the map.

Hiking Etiquette

Most hikers go to the mountains to escape the problems of the city. Let's not bring those same problems to the mountains. Always practice no-trace hiking by using these guidelines.

1. Drive and ride (mountain bikes) only on roads and trails where such travel is allowed; hike only on established trails or paths, on rock, or in washes.

2. Help keep the area clean. Pack out your trash and recycle it, pick up trash even if it's not yours, and dispose of human waste properly. Bury all human waste at least 200 feet from the trail and at least six inches deep.

3. Protect and conserve desert water sources. Carry your own water. Leave pools, potholes, and running water undisturbed.

4. Allow space for wildlife. Teach children not to chase animals.

5. Leave historic sites, Native American rock art, ruins, and artifacts untouched for the future. Admire rock art from a distance. Stay out of ruins and report violations.

Change

Everything in this book is accurate and current, but things change. Trailheads can be relocated, trails can be altered, permit procedures can change, and websites can disappear. However, mountains don't move, even though I had a reader claim they did! My point is, do some research before leaving on that once-in-a-lifetime hiking trip. I've listed numerous websites throughout the book, but who knows how long they'll be around?

Companion Website and Blog

My own website, hopefully, will be around for many more years. It's located athikinglasvegas.com.

Here you'll find more than 360 hikes you can download in PDF format for a small fee. There are photos of hundreds of peaks, slide shows of hikes, and even videos.

I write about hiking news on my blog: hikinglasvegas.blogspot.com/. Well, that's about it. So, dear reader, take a hike!

NEVADA

Introduction to Classic Nevada Hikes

Although most people think of Nevada as nothing but desert, it boasts 314 mountain ranges, the most in the U.S. outside of Alaska. From knife-edge ridges to the highest peak, this book has the best remote hikes in Nevada. Since they're not close to each other, don't plan to do all these hikes in one trip.

Starting at the top, Boundary Peak is the highest in the state. At 13,140 feet, it commands a magnificent view of the Sierra Peaks, which are less than 40 miles away (as the crow flies). Moapa Peak stands near the Arizona boarder and has a knife-edge ridge that will get anyone's attention. Moving to the southern end of the state, Spirit Mountain is the best peak to bag. It overlooks Laughlin, Nevada, where cheap rooms and food await hungry and tired hikers in numerous hotel-casinos. Wheeler Peak is the highest in Great Basin National Park, the least visited national park in the U.S.

I'm not geographically challenged, so I realize Eagle Mountain, and Mopah and Umpah Points, are not in Nevada. They are, however, near the border of Nevada and fit better in this section than in any other. Eagle Mountain rises straight up out of the desert floor. It's the perfect winter hike. Mopah and Umpah Points are dramatic pinnacles that, at first glance, look impossible to climb without ropes. Remember, ropes aren't used for climbing mountains; they're used to hang people you don't like!

I'm pretty sure that's not illegal anymore. Check to be sure.

With the exception of Wheeler, these peaks are in the middle of nowhere. There are no fees, hours, or visitor centers. If you're looking for solitude, these hikes will satisfy. Even Wheeler Peak in Great Basin National Park doesn't have an entrance fee. The Visitor Center is located just north of the town of Baker, NV, on the west side of NV487. Hours are 8 a.m.-4:30 p.m. daily. It's closed November until the end of March. If you have time, Lehman Cave tour is a great experience. More information: www.nps.gov/grba/planyourvisit/lehman-caves-tours.htm.

PHOTO 1

Boundary Peak and Montgomery Peak
Trail and Route

Trailhead: At the end of dirt road, marked
Distance: 8 miles, Boundary Peak; 9 miles, both peaks, up and back
Elevation gain: Boundary, 4,200 feet; both peaks, 4,501 feet
Elevation of peak: Boundary 13,140 feet, Montgomery, 13,441 feet
Time: Boundary, 6–8 hours; both peaks, 7–9 hours, up and back
Difficulty: 5
Danger level: 5
Class: 2 to Boundary Peak; 3 to Montgomery Peak
How easy to follow: 3
Children: No
Waypoints (WGS 84): See page 16
Fees: None
Best season: Summer

Driving Directions

From the town of Dyer, NV, where you can buy gas, set your odometer to zero at the post-office sign (on the right side of the road). Continue another 17.4 miles on NV264 and turn left at the low-to-the-ground Trail Canyon sign. Drive 11 miles and turn right, then follow the road as it curves west (left). BB Mine lies just to the north. Turn right at 12.1 miles. There's a "Trail" sign at the turn. You'll pass a small manmade pond. At 13.7 miles, go left at the fork and continue one mile to the trailhead (Waypoint 1). Your mileage may very slightly.

Comments: Boundary Peak is the highest point in Nevada. Its sister, Montgomery Peak, stands across the imaginary Nevada/California border. From a distance, Boundary Peak is striking. However, once near the summit, it looks more like a pile of rocks on a ridgeline than a peak. In contrast, the closer you get to Montgomery Peak, the more intimidating it looks.

Even in August, it will be cold at night. Come prepared for cold weather if camping. If you're planning to do both peaks, the southern descent along the west side of Boundary Peak can be very cold during the morning hours. It's normal for snow to remain on the route until late-June.

I've given the details of the bad-weather gully descent. If caught in a storm, the gully descent is safer and quicker than the normal descent. It cuts the descent time by about one hour. You should be comfortable on loose scree if you choose this descent route. Photo 1 is Boundary Peak from the trailhead.

Lodging: No motels are nearby. There are no designated campsites. Undeveloped campsites are limited. The parking area at the trailhead is on a grade, making it a poor choice. The best campsite is found about 0.10 of a mile before the trailhead. Water is available in Trail Canyon Creek, which is close by.

The Hike: The trail begins at the kiosk, heads west up Trail Canyon, and passes a trailhead register. It narrows and crosses to the south side of the creek about 400 yards from the trailhead. As the trail pulls away from the creek, the saddle comes into view (see Photo 2).

SADDLE

PHOTO 2

Just beyond this point, you'll hike past a Boundary Peak Wilderness sign.

The trail stays to the south (left) of a dense growth of trees. Once beyond the trees, the trail crosses a soggy section of terrain. When the trail divides, go left. Eventually, the trail braids into dozens of small paths. Continue west through the sagebrush toward the trees. The trail stays on the south (left) side of the drainage. Once in the trees, a path leads to the saddle. Look for cairns on boulders when the path fades. It soon becomes defined again and travels to the saddle. The saddle (Waypoint 2) lies 2.2 miles from the trailhead. At the saddle, you're treated to a vista of the snowcapped Sierra to the west. Take a break, because you have 1,200 feet to gain in less than a half-mile. Follow the obvious trail as it heads SW up the extremely steep slope. A number of use trails develop the higher you climb. The trails stay to the west of the ridge. Eventually, one trail forms, stays well *below* the ridge, and heads toward a mound of talus at a small saddle. The steep north face of Boundary Peak comes into view at the saddle (see Photo 3).

BOUNDARY PEAK

PHOTO 3

Follow the trail as it traverses SE across a west-facing slope. Once across the slope, the trail connects with the main ridgeline. Follow a path SW up the ridge aiming for the pile of talus (see Photo 4). If you get into loose scree, you're too low. Just before the talus, head east and walk over to the other side of the ridge. From here the peak lies 200 to 300 yards SW. Follow the path to the summit (Waypoint 3).

PEAK

PHOTO 4

Congratulations! You're standing at the highest point in Nevada. The highest peak in Nevada also has some of the best views. To the south towers your next objective, Montgomery Peak. Beyond it is White Mountain (14,246 feet). To the west are the snowcapped Sierra. To the north some 6,500 feet below are Queen and Benton valleys. To the east you can see the winding gravel road you drove in on.

From Boundary Peak, Montgomery Peak looks tough. It's actually an easy class 3 climb (see Photo 5). Allow at least 90 minutes to climb Montgomery and return to Boundary. Take a good look at the sky before deciding to climb Montgomery. You should be off both peaks before noon. If you start hiking by 6 a.m., you should be at Boundary Peak by 10 a.m., Montgomery by 11 a.m., and descending before noon.

MONTGOMERY PEAK

PHOTO 5

Start hiking to Montgomery Peak by heading SW down the ridge. Pass the first *major* outcrop to the west (right) and continue down to a saddle. Continue on the ridge to the last outcrop, drop down, and hike along a path on the east (right) side. Start your ascent to Montgomery by climbing back up to the ridge. Stay on the crest of the ridge. Although slightly exposed, the climbing is easy. Once within 150 yards of the peak, the ridge becomes technical. Stay to the east

PHOTO 6

(left) and head up to the peak as shown in Photo 6.

There's no cairn at the peak (Waypoint 4), only an army box containing a register. Comparing the two registers, it's apparent Montgomery Peak is the lesser-climbed peak. To the south lies Middle Canyon, a possible alternate route to Montgomery Peak. Access into Middle Canyon is questionable at this time. The old access road into Trail Canyon, which is in many of the guidebooks, is closed. This appears to be the same road that forks and leads into Middle Canyon.

To Descend: Retrace your steps back to Boundary Peak. Follow the trail off the summit. Once near the pile of talus in Photo 5, head down the west side along the same path on your ascent route. Just beyond this point the ridge splits. You can continue retracing your steps or you can descend the East Ridge. A path begins along the ridge and curves north down the gully.

The path is a pleasant surprise. Follow it all the way into Trail Canyon. Here's how to find the trail and avoid hiking cross-country back to the trailhead. When the path disappears, follow a small ridge *north* toward the middle of the canyon. When the ridge disappears, look east (right) for a large area of grass with a log. The trail lies about 70 yards east near the south (right) slope. Follow the trail east to the trailhead.

WAYPOINTS:
1. 37.8660N / 118.3088W
2. 37.86306N / 118.34602W
3. 37.84610N / 118.35379W
4. 37.83800N / 118.35693W

PHOTO 1

Eagle Mountain
Route

Trailhead: Unnamed gravel road, unmarked
Distance: 3 miles, up and back
Elevation gain: 1,800 feet
Elevation of peak: 3,806 feet
Time: 3 to 4 hours, up and back
Difficulty: 2
Danger level: 3
Class: 3
How easy to follow: 2
Children: No
Waypoints (WGS 84): See page 20
Fees: None
Best season: Winter

Driving Directions

From Las Vegas Blvd., turn west on NV160 (Pahrump Highway). When you pass Rainbow Boulevard, set your odometer to zero. Drive 53 miles, passing through the heart of Pahrump, and turn left (west) on Bell Vista Road. (This is known as the shortcut to Death Valley.) Drive 26 miles on Bell Vista Road. At the stop sign, turn left and drive 8.4 miles to an obscure gravel road on the left side of the road (Waypoint: Road). Look for a cairn marking the turnoff. The gravel road heads north (left). After 0.2 miles, take the left fork. In 0.1 of a mile, take the right fork and park at the Wilderness sign. Waypoint 1 is a little beyond the Wilderness sign.

Note: Your mileage may be slightly different to due tire size and tire pressure.

Comments: This is a great winter hike. The rock is surprisingly good. The last 50 yards are a pseudo knife-edge ridge. The summit has a great view of the snowcapped Telescope Peak. The route is well-cairned. Photo 1 is Eagle Mountain from the trailhead.

PHOTO 2

Lodging: Various hotels and motels in Las Vegas and Pahrump.

The Hike: From the trailhead, immediately cross the Amargosa River (normally dry) and walk NE almost a mile to the start of the drainage in

Photo 2 (Waypoint 2). Veer left, then scramble up the drainage about 300 yards passing Waypoint 3 to a wall at the head of the drainage (Waypoint 4). (Although there's a path in the drainage, hiking on the solid rock is easier.) Follow a path that heads south toward the summit and gains a ridge (Waypoint 5). The ridge offers excellent views out to the east.

PHOTO 3

PHOTO 4

The path weaves to the east side of the mountain. Photo 3 shows the ridge you hike around to the south via the path. Continue to Waypoint 6 where the path fades. Climb the chute and wall in Photo 4 to gain the summit ridge. It's an easy class 3 climb, but it's exposed. Continue over easier rock to the summit (Waypoint 7).

To Descend: Retrace your steps. If you lose the path, you're probably too high.

WAYPOINTS:
Road: 36.20836N / 116.38087W
1. 36.21079N / 116.37791W
2. 36.21498N / 116.36260W
3. 36.21579N / 116.35997W
4. 36.21479N / 116.35942W
5. 36.21404N / 116.35829W
6. 36.21149N / 116.35693W
7. 36.21134N / 116.35650W

PHOTO 1

Moapa Peak
Route

Trailhead: End of dirt road, not marked
Distance: 6.5 miles, up and back
Elevation gain: 3,351 feet
Elevation of peak: 6,471 feet
Time: 6-7 hours, up and back
Difficulty: 5
Danger level: 5
Class: 3
How easy to follow: 4
Children: no
Waypoints (WGS 84): See page 25
Fees: None
Best season: Spring

Driving Directions

From Las Vegas, take Interstate 15 approximately 60 miles to exit 100 (Carp–Elgin). Go left under Interstate 15 for 0.10 of a mile and turn right onto a paved road. In less than 0.10 of a mile, turn left onto an unmarked dirt road. The road goes under two sets of power lines and then forks. Take the right fork. (Don't turn onto the power-line road.) If you don't see a water tank and a corral about 0.30 of a mile beyond the fork, you're on the wrong road. Stay on the main road. It eventually curves to the right and heads for Moapa Peak. Continue on the main road, taking all right-handed forks, until it circles into itself by a rusted water container (Waypoint 1).

There're a few rough spots along the last few miles of the road. **A high-clearance vehicle is needed. This could change if the road worsens over the years.** Although you could drive another quarter-mile up the road, it's best to park where I indicated. This way your car serves as a landmark for the descent. Driving time from Las Vegas is about 90 minutes.

Comments: This hike is for advanced hikers only. The knife-edge ridge is exposed in parts. At one point, you'll have to straddle it, with 100 feet between you and the ground. That being said, if you do this hike, it will become one of your favorites. It's one of the classic hikes in southern Nevada. There are hiker-made paths along the route, but they become obscure. Pick a good day to do this hike. No snow, no wind, and no short days. Late March or early April is normally a good time of the year to do the hike. **Do not attempt the hike if it's hot!**

Lodging: Various deals on hotel rooms in Mesquite. www.visitmesquite.com/mtourism/accommodations/index.jsp.

Camping: No official campsites. You could camp at the trailhead, but there's no water. It's as primitive as it gets. With the great deals on rooms in Mesquite, it's not worth camping for most.

The hike: Continue NW up the road into Jack's Pockets. Once through Jack's Pockets, hike cross-country toward a wash that lies to the west of the peak. You can't see the wash from this point, but keep hiking NW toward a small grayish ridge in Photo 2.

GRAY RIDGE

PHOTO 2

The wash lies on the far (NW) side of the ridge. Once in the wash, follow it as it snakes to the west of the peak. When the wash narrows, find the path on the left bank and follow it passing Waypoint 2. The path soon drops back into the wash. Just beyond that point the wash divides; take the left fork. Follow the wash to the saddle (Waypoint 3).

When you're at the saddle, the peak is to your right (north). Head NW on a faint path about 200 yards to a wall. Once near the wall, look for cairns that mark the way up the class 2 and 3 ledges of the wall (Waypoint 4).

The overall direction up the ledges is NE; however, you'll be doing a lot of switchback climbing.

Traverse about 150 yards NE along a hiker's path. Head north (left) up the slope toward the peak.

Photo 5 was taken along this point showing the peak.

Keep hiking north up this strenuous slope toward the peak. When you come to a low angled wall, stay below it. Two boulders, about 30 yards apart, with cairns on them mark this point. Continue north up a fairly steep slope. At the top of the slope (Waypoint 5), head east toward the sheer wall. A boulder with a cairn marks the start of a path that traverses east along the bottom of the sheer wall. The traverse remains somewhat level for several hundred yards (Waypoint 6) before it starts to ascend. Watch for the wall to end as the path ascends the slope. Head north up the steep slope, following numerous cairns, to the base of the knife-edge ridge. Walk around to the *back* (north) side of the knife-edge ridge (Waypoint 7).

A large cairn marks the

PEAK

PHOTO 5

PHOTO 6

chute that leads to the knife-edge ridge (see Photo 6). Once on the ridge, extreme caution must be taken. The ridge is about 100 yards. If you make it past the first 30 yards, you'll make it to the peak (Waypoint 8).

If this is your first knife-edge ridge, congratulations! You'll find a sign-in book inside an army ammo box. As you'll see when you read the sign-in book, not many people have climbed this peak. The views are outstanding. Your car sits more than 3,000 feet below. You can see it from the peak. To the SE is Lake Mead; to the west stands Mt. Charleston.

To Descend: Retrace your steps. It's easier to follow the paths during the descent. Do not be tempted to descend south too soon along the main traverse. Look for a large cairn just to the south (left) of the path. It marks the end of the traverse.

WAYPOINTS:
1. 36.83449N / 114.44159W Trailhead
2. 36.84613N / 114.45215W
3. 36.85031N / 114.45871W Saddle
4. 36.85176N / 114.4592W Wall and climb
5. 36.85543N / 114.45503W
6. 36.85763N / 114.45116W
7. 36.85927N / 114.44903W Knife edge ridge
8. 36.85866N / 114.45116W Peak

SUMMIT

KNOB

PHOTO 1

Spirit Mountain
Trail and Route

Trailhead: Along Christmas Tree Pass road, unmarked
Distance: 5 miles, up and back
Elevation gain: 2,000 feet
Elevation of peak: 5,639 feet
Time: 4-6 hours, up and back
Difficulty: 3
Danger level: 2
Class: 2 (one very easy class 3 chute)
How easy to follow: 3
Children: No
Waypoints (WGS 84): See page 30
Fees: None
Best time to hike: Winter

Driving Directions

From Las Vegas: From the junction of I-215 and US93, head south on US93 toward Boulder City. Turn right (south) onto US95. Once you pass Cal-Nev-Ari, drive 2.3 miles and turn left on the signed Christmas Tree Pass road. Drive 6.1 miles and veer left when the road forks. Continue 1.0 mile to a large pull-off and road to the left. High-clearance vehicles can drive about 0.4 miles on the side road. All others should park at the pulloff.

From Laughlin: From the intersection of Casino Drive and NV163, turn left (west) on 163 and drive 5.9 miles to the signed Christmas Tree Pass Road. Drive 8.5 miles up Christmas Tree Pass Road to a large pulloff and road on the right. High-clearance vehicles can drive about 0.4 miles up the road. All others should park at the pulloff.

Note: We must have seen 10 police and highway patrol cars on NV95. Make sure to drive the speed limit.

Comments: This is one of the better desert peaks in Nevada. The route description includes the hiker's path, which makes this hike a delight. Without the path this could be a brushy nightmare. You get great views from the peak. On a clear day you can see Charleston Peak and entries in the register go back to the 1960s! A GPS is recommended for this hike.

Lodging: Several casinos in Laughlin have great weekly specials on rooms.

The Hike: From where you parked (Waypoint 1), walk east about 350 yards on the road and across the desert to Waypoint 2, which is just to the right of the knob in Photo 1. Descend NW about 350 yards to the start of an abandoned road (Waypoint 3). You lose about 200 feet in elevation during the descent. Follow the road about 400 yards to a drainage (Waypoint 4) that comes in from the east (right).

Hike in the drainage or through the desert about 200 yards to where the drainage divides (Waypoint 5). Hike through the north (left) fork about 450 yards and exit when you start to see cairns out to the left of the drainage. See Photo 2 for an overview. Several hikers' paths soon converge (Waypoint 6). Follow the path a couple hundred yards to the top of the pass (Waypoint 7). Photo 3 shows the route from the pass. Traverse around the head of a gully via the path. Look for cairns if you lose the path. Continue following the path for almost a mile until you reach the summit ridge (Waypoint 8).

Head west (left) along the summit ridge about 100 yards to the summit (Waypoint 9). You'll climb an easy class 3 chute before reaching the summit (see Photo 4). A register is located inside an ammo box.

PHOTO 3

PHOTO 4

To Descend: Retrace your steps. This is where a GPS becomes useful. You won't see your car until you're almost on it.

Bonus: If you still want to hike, get in your car and drive south 6.7 miles on Christmas Tree Pass road to the signed Grapevine Canyon. Follow the trail from the parking lot to the start of the canyon. There are tons of petroglyphs in the rock at the mouth of the canyon. You can continue another 400 yards or so, paralleling a small creek. Lots of opportunity for photos here. There are bathrooms at the parking lot. Retrace your steps to the trailhead.

WAYPOINTS:
1. 35.26490 N / 114.74356 W
2. 35.26542 N / 114.74023 W
3. 35.26673 N / 114.73680 W
4. 35.26928 N / 114.73413 W
5. 35.26836 N / 114.73266 W
6. 35.26738 N / 114.72887 W
7. 35.26813 N / 114.72781 W
8. 35.27473 N / 114.72251 W
9. 35.27497 N / 114.72334 W

JEFF DAVIS PEAK

WHEELER PEAK

PHOTO 1

Wheeler Peak
Trail

Trailhead: Along Scenic Drive Road, marked
Distance: 8.4 miles, up and back
Elevation gain: 2,902 feet
Elevation of peak: 13,063 feet
Time: 5-7 hours, up and back
Difficulty: 4
Danger level: 4
Class: 1
How easy to follow: 2
Children: No
Waypoints: Not needed
Fees: None
Best season: Summer

Driving Directions

From Las Vegas, take I-15 north 28 miles and turn north (left) onto US93. Drive 260 miles on US93 and turn east (right) onto US6/50. Follow it 34 miles and turn south (right) onto NV487. Drive five miles into Baker and turn west (right) onto NV488. Drive five miles and turn north (right) onto Wheeler Peak Scenic Drive. (The Visitor Center is one more mile on 488.) Drive 11 miles to the signed Summit trailhead parking. Drive time from Las Vegas is five hours.

Comments: Wheeler Peak is the highest peak in Great Basin National Park and the second highest peak in Nevada. About a mile to the east stands Jeff Davis Peak, the second highest peak in the park. Between them, 1,500 feet below, lies Nevada's only glacier. Be sure to drink plenty of water, since you'll be above 10,000 feet the entire hike. Photo 1 is Wheeler Peak.

Lodging: Various campgrounds inside the park are available at $12 per night.

www.nps.gov/grba/planyourvisit/campgrounds.htm

The Hike: The single-track trail heads south at a slight grade as it passes through sagebrush, shrubs, and wildflowers before entering a forest of aspens. In about one mile, the trail merges with the Stella Lake Trail. Continue 0.1 of a mile, where the trails divide. Turn north (right) at the sign for Wheeler Peak. If you want to hike to Stella Lake before hiking to Wheeler Peak, head south (left) on the Stella Lake Trail for 0.1 of a mile to Stella Lake.

Wheeler Peak Trail travels through a meadow, turns south around the head of the basin, and heads toward the SW ridge. At around two miles from the trailhead, Stella Lake comes into view. The grade becomes moderate as the trail uses switchbacks to gain the ridge. The trail curves to the east as it goes above the tree line. There's a good view of the summit ridge along the switchbacks. The switchbacks end at a broad saddle.

From the saddle, you have another two miles of trail and 2,200 feet to gain. The trail continues up the crest of the ridge. Cairns placed strategically among boulders help you stay on course when the trail disappears. The terrain temporarily levels before the final push to the peak. The first windbreak at the summit contains the summit register. Be sure to walk to the east end of the peak for a great view of the glacier.

The peak to the east of the glacier is Jeff Davis Peak. To the north stands Bald Mountain. Farther north and a little east stands the treeless Mt. Moriah Peak; it's not part of the national park. Around the cirque to the south stands the twin peaks of Mt. Baker.

To Descend: Retrace your steps.

UMPAH POINT

MOPAH POINT

PHOTO 1

Mopah and Umpah Points
Route

Trailhead: End of dirt road NS629, unmarked
Distance: 9 miles, both peaks, up and back
Elevation gain: 3,800 feet (both peaks)
Elevation of peaks: 3,530 and 3,553 feet
Time: 6-8 hours, both peaks, up and back
Difficulty: 3
Danger level: 4 (exposure, loose rock, excessive heat)
Class: 4 (one short climb on each peak)
How easy to follow: 4
Children: No
Waypoints (WGS 84): See page 38
Fees: None
Best season: Winter, extreme heat during summer months.

Driving Directions

From the junction of I-215 and US93 in Henderson, NV, head south on 93 toward Boulder City. Turn right (south) onto US95 and drive approximately 90 miles to Needles, California. Veer right onto US95 when it splits from I-40. Continue almost 30 miles to mile marker 22. About 200 yards *beyond* mile marker 22, turn right onto a gravel road (NS629). Drive 4.2 miles to the road's end (Waypoint 1). A high-clearance vehicle is recommended, but it's not a must. Photo 1 is Mopah Point and a sliver of Umpah Point from the trailhead.

Comments: These two peaks are some of the finest desert peaks you'll ever climb. From first sight, they look impossible to climb without ropes. Obviously you can choose to do only one of the peaks, but doing both is certainly doable in one day. The route to Umpah is not the standard route; it's shorter and has more climbing. Camping is allowed at the trailhead. Watch out for catclaw.

Lodging: Various hotels and motels in Needles, CA.
hotel-guides.us/california/needles-ca-hotels.html

Camping: At the trailhead. No permit needed, no amenities; bring water.

The Hike: From the metal fence, hike west on the continuation of the dirt road about 0.75 of a mile where it ends at the remnants of a stone cabin. Hike SW up a wash about 2 miles. There are numerous hikers' paths in the wash that avoid brush. When the view of Mopah comes back into sight, leave the wash (Waypoint 2) and hike cross-country to the notch in Photo 2.

PHOTO 2

Stay near the east wall to avoid drainages as you make your way to the notch. Once at the notch, head south over easy terrain to a second notch, see Photo 3 (Waypoint 3).

PHOTO 3

From the second notch, veer right and into a large gully. Follow a path and cairns to the wall in Photo 4. Veer right onto a wide ledge and continue roughly 60 yards to an alcove and the class 3 climb in Photo 5. Once past the climb, hike about 50 yards over easy terrain to the narrow chute in Photo 6. Be careful of loose rock as you climb the chute and squeeze through the upper end. Climb down 10 feet from the top of the chute to the class 4 wall in Photo 7. There's exposure here! (The webbing seen in Photo 7 might not be there.) Walk the exposed, but fairly wide, ledge to easy rock (Waypoint 4). Head west about 150 yards over easy rock to the summit (Waypoint 5). A register is found in an ammo box.

PHOTO 4

PHOTO 5

PHOTO 6

To Descend Back to the Trailhead: Retrace your steps. Some might want a belay or hand line for the down climb in Photo 7.

Umpah Point: To continue to Umpah Point, descend the route you ascended to the large gully just before the second notch. Keep descending the gully (Waypoint 6), passing the notch, and move south (right) to large boulders where footing is better.

Soon Umpah Point comes into view and you can see the route (see Photo 8). Head down the final part of Mopah (Waypoint 7) and walk south across the desert to the start of Umpah. Hike up an obvious wash on the north face of Umpah (Waypoint 8). When the wash divides, take the right fork. Continue to the headwall in Photo 9. Climb as seen in the photo or walk to the right for easier rock. Veer left on easier rock to a gully. The best rock is found along the right side of the gully. Continue to the top of the gully (Waypoint 9). Climb the ridge that begins at the top of the gully to the summit block in Photo 10 (Waypoint 10). From here the route traverses and climbs the north face to the summit.

Continue up toward the summit and look for a cairn marking an easy chute to get past difficulties. Once up the rock forces you to the crack in Photo 11. Climb the crack (class 4); get on top of the blocks and scramble east (left) over easy rock to the summit. When I was on the summit, there was no register.

To Descend: Retrace your steps back down to the base of the mountain. Hike north across the desert passing the east face of Mopah. Continue to the wash. Hike NW in the wash to the stone cabin and the road. Follow the road back to the trailhead.

PHOTO 7

PHOTO 8

PHOTO 9

PHOTO 10

PHOTO 11

WAYPOINTS (WGS 84):

1. 34.33526N / 114.72217W
2. 34.31641N / 114.76114W
3. 34.30956N / 114.76351W
4. 34.31087N / 114.76491W
5. 34.3105N / 114.76515W
6. 34.30905N / 114.76288W
7. 34.30723N / 114.76121W
8. 34.30105N / 114.76286W
9. 34.29782N / 114.76332W
10. 34.29777N / 114.76406W
11. 34.29749N / 114.76488W

Introduction to Red Rock Canyon

When you were a kid, did you like solving mazes? Did you yearn for a life-size maze with all the twists and turns? Well, you're in luck. Red Rock Canyon is such a maze and it's only 20 miles west of Las Vegas.

Comprising nearly 200,000 acres of multicolored sandstone, ancient limestone, canyons, peaks, washes, and waterfalls, Red Rock is an outdoor playground waiting to be explored. Actually, I did the exploring so that you can hike some of the wildest routes in the Southwest. This is rock scrambling at its best! There are no long approaches, loose terrain, or bears to deal with. Once you try rock scrambling, normal hiking will seem boring and you'll be converted.

If you're new to rock scrambling, Juniper Peak is a great introductory hike. The route travels by the 1,200-foot Rainbow Wall. The hike to Black Velvet Peak passes by a 2,000-foot wall, on top of which you'll eventually be standing, looking down—you guessed it—2,000 feet. From a distance, the route up Bridge Mountain looks dead vertical and totally insane.

Speaking of insane, wait until you tiptoe out to the summit of White Pinnacle Peak. It's 400 feet straight down to the left and more than a 1,000 feet down to the right. Oh, and there are no chains. It makes Angels Landing look like a walk in the park. And then there's Mt. Wilson, the highest sandstone peak in Red Rock. It's an all-day hike for most, but the effort is well worth it.

Because all the trailheads are located in different areas of Red Rock, make sure to read the driving directions. Bridge Mountain and Juniper Peak hikes are subject to the Scenic Loop Road hours, which are basically sunup to sunset. The other hikes aren't, but you never want to descend these routes in the dark.

The area is managed by the BLM and is home to bighorn sheep, mountain lions, deer, and burros. Permits aren't required for hiking. The Red Rock Visitor Center, located at the start of the Scenic Loop Road, is open seven days a week from 8:30 a.m. to 4:30 p.m. Red Rock Canyon is on Pacific Time.

I consider Red Rock Canyon my backyard. I've named more than two dozen peaks and found over 50 routes. If you like hiking in Red Rock, check out my website, hikinglasvegas.com, where you'll find an additional 120 hiking and scrambling routes in Red Rock Canyon.

Tips: While hiking keep your eyes open for bighorn sheep, the acrobats of the mountains. I have seen them on about half the hikes I have done.

The best type of shoes/boots for hiking in Red Rock are those with Stealth Rubber soles. They stick to the sandstone better than any other type of sole.

BLACK VELVET PEAK

PHOTO 1

Black Velvet Peak
Route

Trailhead: Black Velvet parking area, not marked
Distance: 8 miles loop hike
Elevation gain: 2,288 feet
Elevation of peak: 6,234 feet
Time: 6-8 hours, up and down
Difficulty: 5
Danger level: 5
Class: 3
How easy to follow: 5
Children: No
Waypoints (WGS 84): See page 49
Fees: None
Best season: Spring and autumn

Driving Directions

From the Las Vegas Strip, head south and turn right (west) onto NV160 (Blue Diamond Highway). Drive 15.3 miles on 160 and turn right onto an unmarked paved road on the right. (If you pass mile marker 16, you've gone too far.) Just past the bathrooms, the road changes to gravel. Drive 1.9 miles to a gate. Make a left just before the gate and follow the road 0.7 miles to Black Velvet parking area (Waypoint 1). If coming from NV159, turn right onto 160 and drive 4.6 miles to the paved road. Photo 1 is Black Velvet Peak.

Comments: Quite simply, this is one of the best hikes in Red Rock Canyon. Black Velvet Wall towers almost 2,000 feet. You'll hike past the base of the wall and stand at the top of the wall looking down 2,000 feet to the canyon you hiked through. A GPS is recommended to follow this route.

Lodging: Numerous hotels in Las Vegas. Red Rock Resort is the closest.

Camping: Red Rock Campground, $10 per night. Very sparse. www.blm.gov/nv/st/en/fo/lvfo/blm_programs/blm_special_areas/red_rock_nca/recreation/red_rock_campground.html

The Hike: Follow the obvious but unsigned gravel road as it heads west toward Black Velvet Canyon. The road forks in a couple hundred yards; take the right fork, which narrows to a single-track trail. When the trail forks again, follow the left fork, which soon goes across red dirt before descending into the wash (Waypoint 2). Scramble through the wash about 300 yards until you see a class 5 30-foot dry fall. To bypass the dry fall, go left and follow a path that leads to the start of the exposed third class ledges (see Photo 2). These are the famous Black Velvet Ledges, exposed, but an easy class 3.

PHOTO 2

PHOTO 3

Once above the ledges, drop back into the wash and boulder *several hundred* yards up the canyon encountering several class 3 sections. When the canyon divides (Waypoint 3—a little before the divide), go west (left) into the largest fork (see Photo 3). Scramble about 300 yards up this steep *sandstone* canyon (it will feel much longer) to the 50-foot log in Photo 4. You'll leave the wash at this point. Head south up the steep dry waterfall, which can be seen behind the log in Photo 4.

Up to this point, the route was easy to follow. Now it becomes tricky in certain places. Look for cairns if you lose the route.

PHOTO 4

PHOTO 5

Scramble up the waterfall toward the three trees in Photo 5 (Waypoint 4). A 40-foot wall sits about 50 yards behind the trees. To get to the top of the wall, go right along the bottom of the wall, to a point where you can climb the six-foot wall in Photo 6.

Hike south along the sandstone ledge in Photo 7 to a *faint* path that travels up loose red-chipped sandstone. At the top (Waypoint 5), you'll see Black Velvet Peak and two other un-named peaks (see Photo 8).

From here, you'll walk along the famous Keystone Thrust Fault. Notice how the terrain

PHOTO 6

PHOTO 7

changed from sandstone to limestone. Follow the path as it goes around the heads of Black Velvet Canyon. The path traverses without gaining or losing much elevation. You past Waypoints 6 and 7 as you follow the path. It becomes hard to follow at times, but keep heading toward the peaks.

Once you're within about 100 yards of the first peak, you'll descend (Waypoint 8) to a section of reddish dirt and rock. Photo 9 shows the route *around* the first peak.

The route becomes harder to follow from the reddish dirt to just beyond the first peak. Look for cairns. Hike NE out on the white sandstone until you can easily climb off to the north (left) (Waypoint 9). Go north about 25 yards to a wall with black varnish at the bottom (see Photo 10). Turn west (left) and hike up the brushy slot to a dropoff. About 15 feet *before* the slot ends, find a hole on the right. Squeeze through the hole.

Once up (Waypoint 10), walk NE toward the first peak. There's a huge

BLACK
VELVET PEAK   2ND PEAK   1ST PEAK

PHOTO 8

1ST PEAK

2ND PEAK

PHOTO 9

PHOTO 10

drop-off to your left. Walk about 50 yards until you come to the head of the drop-off. Go north (left) climbing over boulders. You're now on the other side of the drop-off. A few yards ahead off to the right is what appears to be a very tricky traverse (see Photo 11). It's not as bad as it looks. Once past the traverse, the second peak comes into view. You're now past the first peak (see Photo 12).

2ND PEAK

PHOTO 11

From here, your direction of travel is obvious. Approach the second peak, which is the highest peak, from the south side. Scramble along the *crest* of the ridge (Waypoint 11). There are two short down climbs before reaching the peak (Waypoint 12).

This peak doesn't have the stunning views of Black Velvet Peak; however, there's a sign-in book. To the north about 200 yards and 100 feet less in elevation stands Black Velvet Peak.

Continue east along the same ridge 15 yards to a large cairn and path that leads to Black Velvet Peak. Go north (left) on the path and descend the slope toward Black Velvet Peak. Once at the low point, scramble up to Black Velvet Peak (Waypoint 13).

You made it! You can admire the view from here, but for an awesome view head NW toward the very top of Black Velvet Canyon Wall. You're looking down 2,000 feet at the canyon you were hiking through early in the day. You might see climbers on the wall.

To Descend: If you don't have a GPS, make a note of the time. This will help you find the path that travels down the ridge. Start by heading south retracing your steps back up to the *same ridgeline* near the second peak. Veer slightly SE as you climb onto the ridgeline. Once on the ridge, hike east several hundred yards. There's an occasional path and numerous cairns. Veer south (right) of the first peaklet you come to. Again, head south (right) to avoid climbing to a second peaklet. Once past the peaklet, head up to the ridgeline and pick up the path as it heads east. Now, look at your watch. Once 25 minutes has past since you left Black Velvet Peak, start looking for a path that heads north (left) down the slope. It's marked by two large cairns and a third cairn off to the left. Also, a log sits about 10 yards down the slope next to the path (Waypoint 14).

The path heads north toward Whiskey Peak, which lies about 600 feet below. The path is easy to follow and well-cairned. About halfway down to the desert floor, the path stops descending and starts traversing due north. Look to your left for large cairns marking the traverse. In about 150 yards Whiskey Peak comes into view. From that point, you'll be scrambling down class 2/3 sandstone. Descend into the gully that lies *before* Whiskey Peak. Go to the north side of the gully and pick up the path that weaves NE toward the desert floor. Luckily, numerous paths all avoid the brush and are easy to navigate. About halfway down, the main path leaves the gully, heads north (left), and traverses a reddish alluvial fan. When the path divides, head down the switchbacks; don't continue north on the path. (You'll end up back in the canyon.) Make sure to descend an easy class 2 chute. Follow the path down to the desert floor. When the path intersects the main trail, go east (right) following it back to your car.

WAYPOINTS:
1. 36.03452N / 115.44966W
2. 36.03600N / 115.46224W
3. 36.04117N / 115.47472W
4. 36.04075N / 115.47991W
5. 36.03924N / 115.47951W
6. 36.03678N / 115.47909W
7. 36.03569N / 115.47864W
8. 36.0336N / 115.47647W
9. 36.03367N / 115.47476W
10. 36.03389N / 115.47462W
11. 36.03373N / 115.47051W
12. 36.03364N / 115.4699W
13. 36.03459N / 115.46876W
14. 36.0311N / 115.46504W

PHOTO 1

Bridge Mountain via North Peak Wash
Route

Trailhead: Along Rocky Gap Road, not marked
Distance: 7 miles, up and back
Elevation gain: 3,330 feet
Elevation of peak: 6,940 feet
Time: 5-7 hours, up and back
Difficulty: 4
Danger level: 3
Class: 3
How easy to follow: 4
Children: No
Waypoints (WGS 84): See page 58
Fees: $7 per car; $30 for a yearly pass. Golden Eagle Pass accepted.
Best season: Spring and autumn

Driving Directions

From the Mirage on Las Vegas Boulevard (the Strip), go north three miles and turn left (west) onto Charleston Boulevard. Drive 16 miles on Charleston/NV159 to Red Rock Canyon. Turn right into Red Rock Canyon. The signed turnoff for Willow Springs is located 7.3 miles past the fee booth on the Scenic Loop Road. It's 0.6 of a mile drive on the paved road to the start of the unsigned Rocky Gap Road, a rough road. Walk, or drive a high-clearance

4WD vehicle 2.4 miles along the Rocky Gap Road and park off to the right (Waypoint 1).

Comments: Bridge Mountain is the crown jewel in Red Rock Canyon. From any angle it looks impossible to climb without using ropes. This route takes you around the vast Ice Box Canyon with 1,000-foot vistas down into the depths of the canyon. You'll cross the famous Keystone Thrust where the younger sandstone lies on top of the older limestone. This is a must-do route for any serious peak bagger. Look for two black lines marking the route beginning at the first chute. Do not attempt this hike in high winds.

Lodging: Numerous hotels in Las Vegas. Red Rock Resort is the closest.

Camping: Red Rock Campground, $10 per night. Very sparse. www.blm.gov/nv/st/en/fo/lvfo/blm_programs/blm_special_areas/ red_rock_nca/recreation/red_rock_campground.html

The Hike: Continue south on the Rocky Gap Road almost a half-mile (it's faster to walk than drive) to the North Peak Wash. It will be to your left, see Photo 1 (Waypoint 2). The North Peak Wash is a strenuous scramble with 1,300 feet of elevation gain in 1,100 yards and two class 3 dry waterfalls. Approach and climb both waterfalls from the left side. As you ascend the North Peak Wash, you cross from limestone to sandstone marking the Keystone Thrust, where younger sandstone lies on top of the older limestone. Make sure to stay in the main wash; don't veer into the south-heading forks.

The top of the wash is known as "Top of the Escarpment" (Waypoint 3). The terrain levels out here and you have a good view of North Peak, which looks more like a bump than a peak from this angle.

PHOTO 2

Head SE 125 yards to the Orange Boulder in Photo 2 (Waypoint 4). At the boulder you can see Bridge Mountain out to the east (left). From this point you'll hike south around various forks of Ice Box Canyon before intersecting the traditional route to Bridge Mountain.

Descend south off of the sandstone and follow a hiker's path about 1,200 yards to the reddish-brown sandstone bowl that sits at the top of a fork of Ice Box Canyon. This bowl is visible from the orange boulder (see Photo 3). You have a great view into Ice Box Canyon along the bowl. A hike climbs out of Ice Box Canyon and up this bowl. See my website for the route.

PHOTO 3

Once across the bowl, descend off the east (left) side (Waypoint 5). Hike south into a red-bottom slickrock wash. You next key landmark is the red crag in Photo 4. Eventually, you'll come to the last fork of Ice Box Canyon (Waypoint 6). Go to the west (right) to get around it. Once past this fork, head NE across the sandstone. Make sure to stay about 50 yards *below* the red crag in Photo 4. Photo 5 provides an overview of the next part of the route. Just beyond the crag, you'll descend onto a shoulder that leads to Bridge Mountain.

PHOTO 4

PHOTO 5

From here, you'll head toward Bridge Mountain by climbing down the shoulder to a bench. You can't veer too far off course because of the sheer drop-offs on either side. Look for cairns to help keep you on course.

The first part of the route *across the shoulder* is flat with numerous and somewhat confusing cairns marking the way. Just keep heading toward Bridge Mountain. The second part of the route descends nearly 300 feet and is well-marked. You have to navigate three chutes to make this 300-foot descent. Photo 6 shows the first chute (Waypoint 7). Follow cairns and black lines past the manzanita to a pinion that marks the top of the second chute (class 3) as seen in Photo 7. Once down, hike 20 to 30 yards heading directly for Bridge Mountain and scramble down the third chute. About 10 yards beyond the chute, down climb the final wall (class 3). You've descended the shoulder.

PHOTO 6

Hike NE across the bench to the base of Bridge Mountain (Waypoint 8). The base is a safe place to leave hikers who are having second thoughts. Photo 8 shows an overview of the first part of the climb.

PHOTO 7

Follow the yellow lines up the crack. If it's windy stay in the crack; otherwise, climb out of the crack to the right and up the beehive sandstone as indicated by the yellow arrows. People who have a fear of heights should stay in the crack. The climb outside of the crack is exposed. Staying in the crack is more protected, but it's a harder climb.

When the beehive sandstone levels, a line of rocks directs you west (left). Step over the crack, follow the ledge 10 yards, turn north (right), and

PHOTO 8

PHOTO 9

scramble up the sandstone 75 yards to the natural bridge (see Photo 9). On the other side of the bridge (arch), a giant ponderosa pine leans against the sandstone. This is a great area to take a break and photos.

Go under the bridge and friction climb along the left wall. A log lies near the wall. At the top of the bridge the dome-shape peak of Bridge Mountain can be seen. Go SE across the sandstone rim and around the Hidden Forest.

The final ascent heads NE along a steep ramp, which is well marked with cairns (see Photo 10). At the top of the ramp, head south 40 yards to the peak (Waypoint 9). A cairn with a sign-in book inside an ammo box marks the peak. A natural shelter lies just below the peak. This is a good place to have lunch and escape the wind. The view from the peak is awesome.

SUMMIT

PHOTO 10

PHOTO 11

To Descend: Retrace your steps back to the Top of the Escarpment (Waypoint 3). From here you can descend the steep North Peak Wash or hike down the North Peak Path. The path is much easier on the knees. If you choose to hike the path, start by descending down to the ridge in Photo 11, where the North Peak Path begins (Waypoint 10). A large cairn marks the path if the wind hasn't blown it down.

Follow the path down the sandstone looking for cairns. Once the path enters the limestone, it's very easy to follow and you'll be able to see your car. The path ends where you parked you car (Waypoint 1).

WAYPOINTS:
1. 36.15165N / 115.52335W Park
2. 36.14627N / 115.52433W Leave Road
3. 36.14308N / 115.51418W Top of the Escarpment
4. 36.14216N / 115.51378W Orange Rock
5. 36.13468N / 115.51455W Descend off bowl
6. 36.13116N / 115.51625W Last fork of Ice Box Canyon
7. 36.13084N / 115.5093W 1st Chute
8. 36.13219N / 115.50566W Base of Bridge Mountain
9. 36.13188N / 115.50163W Summit
10. 36.14398N / 115.51669W Start of North Peak Path

ARNIGHT TRAIL SYSTEM

Destination	Distance one-way
ARNIGHT TRAIL:	1.6 miles, moderate
KNOLL TRAIL HEAD:	.6 mile, easy
OAK CREEK, KNOLLS,	
ARNIGHT LOOP:	3.5 miles, moderate
ESCARPMENT BASE TRAIL:	5.2 miles, difficult

PHOTO 1

Juniper Peak
Route

Trailhead: Oak Creek Canyon, marked
Distance: 6 miles, up and back
Elevation gain: 2,109 feet
Elevation of peak: 6,109 feet
Time: 4-6 hours, up and back
Difficulty: 3
Danger level: 3
Class: 3
How easy to follow: 5
Children: No
Waypoints (WGS 84): See page 64
Fees: $7 per car; $30 for a yearly pass. Golden Eagle Pass accepted.
Best season: Spring and autumn

Driving Directions

From the Mirage on Las Vegas Boulevard (the Strip), drive north 3 miles and turn west (left) onto Charleston Boulevard. Drive 16 miles to Red Rock Canyon. The signed turn-off for Oak Creek Canyon is located 12.2 miles past the fee booth. Turn right and drive 0.70 of a mile on an excellent gravel road to the parking lot.

Comments: This hike has plenty to offer: a trail to warm up on, bouldering through a magnificent canyon, and class 2 and 3 scrambling. Great views of Rainbow Wall, Brownstone Wall, and an awesome overlook into the south fork of Pine Creek make this one of the best hikes in Red Rock Canyon. For people who mainly hike on trails, this route will test your navigational skills. Use common sense.

Lodging: Numerous hotels in Las Vegas. Red Rock Resort is the closest.

Camping: Red Rock Campground, $10 per night. Very sparse. www.blm.gov/nv/st/en/fo/lvfo/blm_programs/blm_special_areas/ red_rock_nca/recreation/red_rock_campground.html

The Hike: Head west on the signed Arnight Trail (see Photo 1), passing a shallow wash around a half-mile. Continue on the trail another quarter-mile and turn SW (left) onto a prominent path (Waypoint 1), which heads straight for Juniper Canyon. Follow this path about 200 yards until it intersects a prominent trail. Go right 15 yards and turn left onto another path. Follow this path about 100 yards to a major fork and turn right, heading for the enormous boulder in Photo 2. (The boulder is also a landmark during the hike back to the trailhead.) The path passes the boulder, then drops into a wash. Go left in the wash, walk 10 yards, turn right, and follow a steep path up and out of the wash. When the path intersects another trail, turn left, walk about 15 yards, and turn left onto the unsigned Juniper Canyon Path. Follow this path a few hundred yards to a fork. Take the right fork, which heads for Juniper Canyon. (If you miss this turn, you'll soon be heading east toward the trailhead.) After a few hundred yards, the path climbs a hill and then parallels a wash coming from Juniper Canyon (Waypoint 2). You'll

PHOTO 2

scramble over a few boulders before the path dead-ends in the wash.

Climb the huge boulders in front of you (class 3) and follow cairns as you weave through the wash. Stay in the main wash watching for cairns. After about 100 yards, the wash narrows and becomes much steeper. At the top of the wash, head right onto a hiker's path. Traverse 25 yards to level ground passing by a fallen log (Waypoint 3). Continue on the well-defined path about 300 yards to a two-foot-high boulder (Waypoint 4).

The path divides here; take the right fork and follow it 10 yards into another wash. Go west (left) in the wash about 30 yards to an opening in the brush where a path starts. It will be to your right (see Photo 3).

PHOTO 3

Hike 30 yards up the steep path to a small boulder field. Head SW through the boulder field (Waypoint 5), aiming for a large blackface boulder at the far side of the boulder field. A cairn sits on top of the boulder (see Photo 4). Just to the right and a little beyond the boulder, the path resumes, then travels 30 yards and empties out onto white sandstone. The reddish-brown towering wall is Brownstone Wall.

The next part of the route parallels Brownstone Wall to a gully, your next major landmark. The gully is located at the north end of Brownstone Wall and lies below the two "Turtle boulders" in Photo 5.

PHOTO 4

PHOTO 5

Scramble NW toward the Turtle boulders. You'll be on slabs of sandstone and hikers' paths as you make your way to the gully below the Turtle boulders. This part of the route is very well-cairned. The hiking is

PHOTO 6

PHOTO 7

mostly class 1 and 2. Once near the Turtle boulders, follow a path that cuts through the manzanita and ends at a juniper tree. Just behind the juniper lies a low point in a sandstone wall. Climb the wall (class 3) and scramble up the small chute (class 3) in Photo 6. You're now just below the Turtle boulders.

Hike west up the beehive sandstone until it becomes too steep. Veer north (right) and hike to the top of the gully, where a fantastic overlook 1,000 feet down into the south fork of Pine Creek stands just to the north (right, Waypoint 6). From here, you're only 10 minutes from the peak.

From the top of the gully, head south (left), passing the second of three large ponderosa pines. Traverse east (left) about 25 yards on sandstone ledges marked by *numerous cairns*. The route makes a 180-degree turn and heads west. Climb off the sandstone ledge and under the boulder in Photo 7. Hike 30 yards to the large pinion pine tree. Turn left (SE) and hike 20 yards going between two small sandstone crags to the boulder that marks Juniper Peak (Waypoint 7).

You made it. Make sure to sign the register. Across Juniper Canyon stands Cloud Tower, a 1,200-foot-high pillar capped with crimson rock. If you look real hard, you might see climbers on the NE face of Cloud Tower. Just to the right of Cloud Tower stands the impressive 1,200 foot Rainbow Wall.

To Descend: Retrace your steps.

WAYPOINTS:
1. 36.11686N / 115.47965W
2. 36.11432N / 115.48869W
3. 36.11362N / 115.49044W
4. 36.11356N / 115.49284W
5. 36.11365N / 115.49343W
6. 36.11703N / 115.49410W
7. 36.11663N / 115.49451W

PHOTO 1

Mt. Wilson
Route

Trailhead: First Creek, marked
Distance: 8.5 miles, up and back
Elevation gain: 3,420 feet
Elevation of peak: 7,070 feet
Time: 7-9 hours, up and back
Difficulty: 5
Danger level: 3
Class: 3
How easy to follow: 5
Children: No
Waypoints (WGS 84): See page 74
Fees: None
Best season: Spring and autumn

Driving Directions   From the Mirage on Las Vegas Boulevard (the Strip), go north three miles and turn left (west) onto Charleston Boulevard. Drive 21 miles on Charleston (it becomes NV159) to the signed First Creek parking area on the right (west) side of the road (Waypoint TH). You don't drive on the Scenic Loop Road to access the trailhead.

Comments: This is one of the most difficult hikes in Red Rock Can-

COTTONWOOD TREE

PHOTO 1

yon. The ascent up the Hidden Bowl is very strenuous, but the views from Mt. Wilson are the most dramatic in Red Rock. I've named some key landmarks to make it easier to follow the route. The route through the canyon depends on the time of year, amount of water in the wash, your climbing ability, and the grapevines. Get a very early start; you don't want to descend in the dark. Your starting time isn't limited to the Scenic Loop hours, since the trailhead is along NV159. The route is cairned. *I highly recommend you use a GPS to follow this route.*

Tip: Due to break ins at the trailhead, make sure to leave valuables at home or take them with you.

Lodging: Numerous hotels in Las Vegas. Red Rock Resort is the closest.

Camping: Red Rock Campground, $10 per night. Very sparse. www.blm.gov/nv/st/en/fo/lvfo/blm_programs/blm_special_areas/red_rock_nca/recreation/red_rock_campground.html

The Hike: Follow the signed trail west toward the mouth of First Creek Canyon. At about a mile and a half, the trail narrows to single-track width. Continue as the trail descends slightly and passes near large scrub oak trees. From this point the trail divides into numerous paths. Follow any path that stays near the creek. Just before the path enters the creek, take the south (left) fork, which climbs a hill. At the top of the hill, the path merges with other paths. Continue west toward the canyon. When the path divides at a 20-foot juniper, follow the north (right) fork down a small hill. At the bottom of the hill, a log has fallen across the path. Eventually, the path goes across a band of red sandstone (Waypoint 1). About 15 feet after the path changes back to dirt, it forks. Take the north (right) fork. If you continue straight, the path soon ends in brush.

The path weaves between two boulders, then heads west (left) into the canyon. Follow the path through the brush and scramble up a large low-angled boulder. Continue on the path and scramble up the boulders to the large cottonwood tree in Photo 1. You're finally in the wash (Waypoint 2).

From here to where you leave the canyon, I'll point out key landmarks that you should pass while bouldering in the wash. Look for footprints in the gravel and cairns to keep you on route. Boulder through the wash past numerous class 3 sections. About 250 yards from where you entered the wash, you'll come to an enormous boulder. Climb as shown in Photo 2 or veer left and scramble up to a path, then back into the wash.

Continue through the wash about 100 yards to what's called the maze; giant boulders create a hole you scramble through (see Photo 3).

The *wash* divides twice (not the canyon); both times go into the left forks, which are free of brush. Soon after the second divide, you'll hike alongside the south (left) wall of the canyon until the wash narrows and you come to the chimney in Photo 4.

The chimney is an easy class 3 climb. At the top of the chimney, a 100-foot dead tree leans against the north side of the wash. The canyon divides just beyond the tree. Hike NW into the right fork of the canyon. *Hikers encounter brush in this fork, because they stay in the fork too long.* Boulder about 40 yards up this fork to an obvious opening through the brush on the west (left) side; see Photo 5 (Waypoint 3).

PHOTO 4

PHOTO 5

PHOTO 6

Once through the opening, continue straight a couple hundred yards in the "Brush-Free" wash (locally named) to the start of the sometimes dry "Cascading Waterfall;" see Photo 6 (Waypoint 4). Scramble up and traverse the north (right) wall to a large ponderosa pine at the top of the cascading waterfall. It's a great place to take a break.

Continue up the wash about 70 yards to a large cairn along the north (right) side of the wash. Leave the wash by scrambling NE (right) up the low-angled slab in Photo 7 (Waypoint 5).

Scramble 30 yards up the slab in Photo 7 and turn left, climbing a crack. Follow the crack 10 *feet*, turn right, and follow the crack as it passes between two scrub oak bushes. Once beyond the scrub oak, traverse right 20 yards along a small ledge to a cairn. Continue traversing until you go around a corner and the terrain opens up. The traverse is well-cairned (see Photo 8).

Head 75 yards up the steep slab of sandstone to

PHOTO 7

the black section of sandstone circled in Photo 9. Continue 20 yards beyond the black section of sandstone to the top. You've climbed out of the
canyon; you now have to drop into the Hidden Bowl. Unfortunately, you
have to lose elevation before ascending the Bowl.

Head NW up the shoulder as seen in Photo 10 (Waypoint 6). The
Hidden Bowl becomes visible from the ridge. From the top of the ridge
descend the ramp about 40 feet and make a hard left onto a wide sandstone ledge (see Photo 11).

PHOTO 10

PHOTO 11

Follow cairns and a path though brush to the start of the bowl (Waypoint 7). Unfortunately, a class 5 dry fall lies ahead. You must go around to the east (right) to get above the dry fall. Traverse across the bowl and then up and left as seen in Photo 12.

You cross Waypoint 8 at the top of a short climb up a boulder. Walk across sandstone and then follow a path around the east side of the dry fall. The good news is you're now above the dry fall (Waypoint 9); the bad news is it gets very strenuous from here.

Ascend easy ramps and move east (right) to the eastern part of the bowl. Photo 13 shows the eastern section of the bowl (Waypoint 10). Ascend NE almost 200 yards up the steep section of the bowl before hiking NW (left) Waypoint 11 to avoid a near vertical wall ahead.

Follow cairns up the broken sandstone to the ramp in Photo 14 (Way-point 12). Continue up steep sandstone to the right of the alcove as seen in Photo 15 to the top of the bowl (Waypoint 13).

PHOTO 12

PHOTO 13

PHOTO 14

You've just gained more than 1,500 feet in about two-thirds of a mile!

Head NW above the alcove about 200 yards to an awesome vista (Waypoint 14). It's very flat here and normally not windy, the perfect place for lunch. This isn't the peak; however, it's only 15 minutes away.

To reach the peak, hike NW up the hill in Photo 16. Follow a path to the top of the hill and down to the saddle just before the summit. Ascend easy rock to the summit.

Wow! You made it. A small cairn hides the sign-in book; you have to look for it. Take in the views from the highest sandstone peak in Red Rock Canyon. You've just climbed one of the toughest peaks in Red Rock.

To Descend: Retrace your steps. Descending is faster. Look for cairns. Many of the cairns were actually made for the descent. To be safe, you

PHOTO 15

PHOTO 16

should have at least four or more hours of daylight left. This means leaving the peak by 12:30 p.m. if you're doing the hike in late fall or winter.

WAYPOINTS:
TH 36.08134N / 115.44804W
 1. 36.07967N / 115.47847W
 2. 36.081N / 115.48054W Cottonwood Tree
 3. 36.08293N / 115.48729W
 4. 36.08394N / 115.48936W
    Start of scramble to Cascading Waterfall
 5. 36.08455N / 115.49065W Leave wash
 6. 36.08507N / 115.48812W
 7. 36.08697N / 115.48795W Start of the bowl
 8. 36.08688N / 115.48577W
 9. 36.08732N / 115.48562W Above the dry fall
10. 36.0879N / 115.48444W
11. 36.08885N / 115.48308W
12. 36.08928N / 115.4833W Ramp
13. 36.0901N / 115.48208W Top of bowl
14. 36.0917N / 115.48311W Overlook
15. 36.09366N / 115.48395W Summit

WHITE PINNACLE
PEAK

PHOTO 1

White Pinnacle Peak
Route

Trailhead: First Creek, marked
Distance: 5 miles, up and back
Elevation gain: 1,900 feet
Elevation of peak: 5,550 feet
Time: 5-6 hours, up and back
Difficulty: 4
Danger level: 4
Class: 4
How easy to follow: 3
Children: No
Waypoints (WGS 84): See page 78
Fees: None
Best season: Spring and autumn

Driving Directions

From the Mirage on Las Vegas Boulevard (the Strip), go north three miles and turn left (west) onto Charleston Boulevard. Drive 21 miles on Charleston (it becomes NV159) to the signed First Creek parking area on the right side of the road. You don't drive on the Scenic Loop to access the trailhead.

Comments: This is the gnarliest peak in Red Rock and, in fact, one of the most uncivilized peaks in the Southwest. If you're looking for exposure, you've found it. The route has some challenging class 4 climbing. Depending on where you're standing, the gully looks impossible; it isn't. Bring 25 feet of rope or webbing to pass packs up the chimney. Photo 1 is the peak.

Tip: Due to brush along the route, wear long pants.

Lodging: Numerous hotels in Las Vegas.

Camping: Red Rock Campground, $10 per night. Very sparse. www.blm.gov/nv/st/en/fo/lvfo/blm_programs/blm_special_areas/ red_rock_nca/recreation/red_rock_campground.html

The Hike: The trail heads SSW toward the mouth of First Creek Canyon. When the trail divides in about a half-mile, take the south (left) fork; the right fork is blocked off by a row of rocks. Walk about 300 yards to the path as seen in Photo 2 (Waypoint 1).

PHOTO 2

Follow the path about 150 yards crossing above the waterfall (may be dry) and pick up any path heading west toward the canyon. Initially, the closer you stay to the wash, the better the path. Follow the path to the ridge below the gully. Hike the ridge to the start of the gully as seen in Photo 3 (Waypoint 2). It's a little less than two miles from the trailhead to the start of the gully and about 900 feet of elevation gain.

The length of the gully is only 500 yards, but you gain al-

PEAK

GULLY

RIDGE

PHOTO 3

PHOTO 4

BOULDER

PHOTO 5

most 1,000 feet. There's lots of class 3 and some class 4 climbing in the gully. Look for cairns to stay on route. Even though you're in a gully and getting lost is impossible, you need to follow the route to avoid horrible brush. Enter the gully on the right side. In less than 100 yards, the gully forks. Veer left, staying in the more prominent gully. Follow the path that weaves through the brush. When the path leads to a chute filled with brush, look to your left for a cairn and climb the wall. Continue on the path, squeezing by a prickly pear. Just beyond the prickly pear, climb a chute exiting left by stepping on a log. Continue to the class 4 crack in Photo 4. Test the rope before using it to climb the crack. The path resumes and heads left at the top of the crack. Continue up the gully to the major chimney in Photo 5.

This is a wild chimney! Hike under the boulder and climb (class 3) on top of it from the back side. Stem up the wall (class 4) and into the back of the chimney. Be careful of loose rock. Scramble up (class 4) and through the small hole to the right (north). You'll have to take your pack off to fit through the hole. *Be careful of loose rock and dirt.* Use your rope to hoist packs through the hole.

The path resumes cutting through the brush. In about 150 yards, the path ends at a steep sandstone wall. Scramble up the wall (class 3) as seen in Photo 6. Once up, you have a great view of Indecision Peak and First Creek Canyon.

Turn left (east) and get ready for one of those once-in-a-lifetime experiences. Walk the very exposed ridge about 75 yards to the peak (see Photo 7). This summit is beyond cool! It's 400 feet down to the left and over 1,000 feet down to the right.

To Descend: Retrace your steps. Descending the chimney is easier than ascending it. For once, larger people have it easier than smaller hikers. You can hook up a rope by a tree near the top of the chimney, if needed.

PHOTO 6

PHOTO 7

WAYPOINTS:
1. 36.08007N / 115.46454W
2. 36.08203N / 115.47609W

Introduction to Mt. Charleston

Mt. Charleston is part of the Spring Mountains, the mightiest mountain range in southern Nevada. The range gets its name from the numerous springs hidden deep inside the mountains; it borders Las Vegas Valley on the west side and extends for 50 miles. No other major city and mountain range within such close proximity have such a difference in elevation. When you stand on Charleston Peak, you look down almost 10,000 feet to Las Vegas, yet you're only 30 miles from the Strip. Charleston Peak, the highest summit in southern Nevada, is named after Charleston, South Carolina.

The Mt. Charleston Area is home to the bristlecone pine, the oldest living thing on Earth. You'll hike past a 3,000-year-old bristlecone named Raintree on the hike to Charleston Peak (11,918 feet). Mummy Mountain (11,542 feet) is one of the most recognizable peaks in southern Nevada. From US95, it looks like a mummy lying down after a long hard night on the Strip! The hike will give some people their first taste of an easy mountaineering route. Griffith Peak (11,056 feet) has the best views of any summit in southern Nevada. From the summit most of the Charleston Peaks and many of the summits in Red Rock are visible.

As of this writing, Mt. Charleston Area has no fees or restricted hours. Make sure to read the driving directions for each hike. Their trailheads are located on different roads. The area is managed by the U.S. Forestry

Service and is home to at least 30 endemic species. The Visitor Center is located 18.4 miles up NV157 (by the ranger station). Hours are from 10 a.m. to 4 p.m.

Tip: You can hike with your dogs, as long as they're on a leash.

GRIFFITH PEAK

PHOTO 1

Griffith Peak via Harris Springs
Trail and Route

Trailhead: Harris Spring Rd., marked
Distance: 10 miles, up and back
Elevation gain: 2,656 feet
Elevation of peak: 11,056 feet
Time: 5–7 hours, up and back
Difficulty: 3
Danger level: 2
Class: 1
How easy to follow: 1
Children: no
Waypoints (WGS 84): See page 83
Fees: None
Best season: Summer

Driving Directions

From Las Vegas, head north on US95 to NV157. Turn left on 157 and drive 12.7 miles to Harris Springs Road (gravel). Drive 3.2 miles on Harris Springs Road and turn right at the sign for Griffith Peak trailhead. (The sign might be missing.) Follow the gravel road six miles to the trailhead (Waypoint 1). A high-clearance vehicle is needed.

Comments: Griffith Peak has the best views of any summit in Mt.

Charleston. This is a magnificent trail with incredible vistas along much of the hike. It's a must-do hike!

The Hike: The trail starts at an easy pace as it makes its way west toward a saddle that lies between Harris and Griffith Peaks. A stunning view of Lovell Canyon is to the south. The first part of the trail started out as a road built by the CCC in the 1940s. President Roosevelt came to inspect the road and asked the foreman the road's destination. When the foreman said he didn't know, the president ordered the construction stopped. The road dead ends, but the trail keeps going. If you look down to the south, a blue car sits at the bottom of a ravine. Apparently, someone thought the road went somewhere.

The trail stays below and to the south of Harris Peak as it heads toward the saddle and Griffith Peak (see Photo 1). Take a break at the saddle and look northwest for a stunning view of Kyle Canyon. A long rest isn't needed, since you have only gained a few hundred feet in elevation.

The incline increases as the trail starts climbing over the rocky cliffs that stand SW of the saddle. The trail offers great views of Mummy Mountain, Kyle Canyon, and Mary Jane Falls by looking north. At the top of the switchbacks, walk over to the ledge for a great view of Kyle Canyon.

PHOTO 2

The trail heads SW as it makes its way to the base of Griffith Peak. Red Rock Canyon is off to the east (left). The dome-shaped mountain is Bridge Mountain. During the summer months a variety of flowers grow near the trail. Once at the top of the switchbacks, a hill off to the SW is often mistaken as Griffith Peak. Griffith lies behind this hill. The trail flattens out as it winds through an area that suffers from an old forest fire. Past the burnt area, the trail becomes steep as it heads south toward the peak. When the trail empties into a meadow (Waypoint 2), the hike becomes a route and leaves the trail, see Photo 2. (The trail does not travel to the peak.)

This is a steep trek gaining 600 feet in less than 700 yards. There are two hills to climb and then the actual peak. As you climber higher, a hiker's path begins. Once on the path, follow it past gnarly bristlecones to the summit (Waypoint 3).

The wind and lower temperatures make Griffith Peak refreshing in the summer and cold in the winter. The rocks at the peak contain numerous fossils; millions of years ago the entire area was underwater. Look at them, but leave them so others can marvel at ancient history. Charleston Peak stands to the west and Mummy Mountain lies across Kyle Canyon to the north. Back to the SE is Red Rock Canyon. The views don't get any better than this!

To Descend: Retrace your steps.

WAYPOINTS:
1. 36.22020N / 115.59804W
2. 36.23489N / 115.64032W
3. 36.23252N / 115.64610W

PHOTO 1

Charleston Peak
Trail

Trailhead: North Loop Trail, marked
Distance: 22 miles, up and back
Elevation gain: 3,554 feet
Elevation of peak: 11,918 feet
Time: All day or overnight backpack
Difficulty: 5
Danger level: 3
Class: 1
How easy to follow: 1
Children: No
Waypoints: Not needed
Fees: None
Best season: Summer

Driving Directions

From Las Vegas, head north on US95 to NV157. Turn left on 157, drive 17.7 miles, and turn right onto NV158. Drive five miles to the North Loop trailhead sign, which is located on the left (west) side of the road.

Comments: Charleston Peak is the highest point in southern Nevada and the only treeless peak in the region. You must come prepared for this all-day hike. You can do it as a backpack, but there's no water at the primitive campsites. A shorter route begins at Trail Canyon and meets up with the North Loop trail at the junction. This route is 16 miles, round trip. See the last page for details.

Lodging: Numerous hotels in Las Vegas.

Camping: Numerous official campgrounds in Mt. Charleston. www.hikinglasvegas.com/fast1.html

The Hike: The trail starts off at an easy grade, wandering past ponderosa pine, pinion pine, and mountain mahogany. To the east on Angel Peak is a large, white, ball-shape observatory. The trail has a few moderate switchbacks before reaching a plateau, about 1.5 miles from the trailhead. Several bristlecone pines scattered throughout this area indicate you're above 9,000 feet. After 12 moderately steep switchbacks, the trail climbs to 10,200 feet. It then descends 150 feet over the next 0.33 of a mile. Looking west, you can see glimpses of Mummy Mountain. The limestone cliffs of Mummy's Toe hover directly in front of the trail. Raintree, the giant bristlecone pine, is more than 3,000 years old and acts as a dividing point. A wooden sign next to Raintree indicates your options and the distances. Continue another 1.5 miles to the junction of Trail Canyon (see Photo 1).

From the junction, hike the North Loop Trail as it heads NW around Mummy Mountain. The grade is moderate as you enter the dead forest. This "people-caused fire" in the late 1940s burned more than 500 acres. Scattered throughout the dead forest are aspens that turn orange and yellow in the fall. Look to the left (south) for a great view of Kyle

PHOTO 2

Canyon; directly in front looms Charleston Peak (see Photo 2).

About a mile from the junction is Cave Springs (see Photo 3). Water runs into a horse trough and a path goes up to a cave-like overhang above it. The North Loop Trail continues southerly through the dead forest and aspens, as the grade becomes steeper. It makes a horseshoe bend and heads NE before switching back and heading west toward the North Rim Ridge. A little less than a mile from the horseshoe bend, a series of bluffs to the left of the trail offers great views of Kyle Canyon. The aspens disappear up here, since the elevation is more than 10,000 feet.

PHOTO 3

The trail flattens as it heads SW around the series of bluffs. Charleston Peak goes in and out of view as the trail starts to imitate a roller coaster. The trail flattens out again and cuts through a forest of bristlecone pines. Three overlooks to the north (right) offer the first views of the Sisters, Mack's Peak, and McFarland Peak. They also make good campsites. The third overlook also has a great view of Charleston Peak and Kyle Canyon, making this one of the best views in the Mt. Charleston area.

The trail continues in a SW direction as it winds along the base of cliffs. A few short but steep switchbacks bring you to the North Rim Ridge. Plan to spend a few minutes catching your breath while you take in the fantastic view of all the northern mountains of the Mt. Charleston area.

The trail remains flat as it heads SE below Devil's Thumb (see Photo 4). Mt. Charleston comes in and out of view as the trail traverses the rocky ledges. Trees are scarce, since the elevation is higher than 11,000 feet. The trail heads around a few bluffs; it seems to take forever to arrive at the base of Charleston Peak. It makes one switchback and climbs around a final bluff before the near mile-long trek to the peak.

The last part of the trail is a series of steep switchbacks with a 17% grade. It's important to drink plenty of water before and during this section. One cause of altitude sickness is a lack of water!

Congratulations. You're standing at the highest point in southern Nevada. Take a moment to experience the silence, breathe the clean air, and be thankful you're in good enough shape to be standing on the peak. The peak offers a fantastic 360-degree view of southern Nevada, eastern California, and southern Utah. An Army box contains a sign-in book. A dug-out fort is a favorite resting spot before starting back down.

To Descend: Retrace your steps.

Starting the hike from Trail Canyon

Distance: 16 miles
Time: 7–10 hours
Driving directions: From Las Vegas, head north on US95 to NV157. Turn left on 157, drive 20 miles, and veer onto Echo Drive at the hairpin curve. Drive a half-mile to the trailhead sign for Trail Canyon.

The Hike: Follow Trail Canyon Trail two miles to the intersection of the North Loop Trail. Head west (left) on the North Loop Trail. Follow the above directions from the intersection of these two trails.

PHOTO 1

Mummy Mountain
Trail and Route

Trailhead: Trail Canyon, marked
Distance: 8.5 miles, up and back
Elevation gain: 3,732 feet
Elevation of peak: 11,542 feet
Time: 5-7 hours, up and back
Difficulty: 4
Danger level: 2
Class: 2
How easy to follow: 3
Children: No
Waypoints (WGS 84): See page 91
Fees: None
Best season: Summer

Driving Directions

From Las Vegas, head north on US95 to NV157. Turn left on 157, drive 20 miles, and veer onto Echo Drive at the hairpin curve. Drive a half-mile to the trailhead sign for Trail Canyon.

Comments: Mummy Mountain is the second highest peak in Mt. Charleston. This is the perfect beginner's mountaineering route to give you a feel for real mountaineering. If you like this hike, you can shoot for hikes in the High Sierra. From the summit of Mummy Mountain, you can see Red Rock Canyon, Las Vegas, and Lake Mead.

Tip: Hiking poles can help ascending and descending the loose scree slope.

Lodging: Numerous hotels in Las Vegas.

Camping: Numerous official campgrounds in Mt. Charleston.

www.hikinglasvegas.com/fast1.html

The Hike: The trail starts in a northerly direction at a leisurely pace, paralleling a dry creekbed that lies to the west. It winds through thick groves of aspens as it heads toward the North Loop Trail junction. To the east lie the rocky cliffs of Cockscomb Ridge. About a half-mile into the hike, the North Rim Ridge can be seen by looking to the northwest. To the north lies Mummy Mountain.

The grade becomes moderate as the trail switches back through pinion pines. Just past this point, Charleston Peak can be seen by looking to the west (left). The trail flattens out briefly, then climbs a small hill as it heads due east toward Cockscomb Ridge. Continue a short distance to the junction of North Loop Trail.

From the junction, the North Loop Trail heads NW (left). A half-mile from the junction, you pass Cave Springs, a year-round source of water. A pipe carries water into a horse trough. Continue on the trail as it weaves through the aspens. The trail leaves the aspens and switchbacks across a scree slope. About 60 yards along the second switchback (about 1.25 miles from the junction), you leave the trail and head north up the scree slope; see Photo 1 (Waypoint 1). The scramble up the scree slope gains almost 600 feet in elevation. At the top of the slope, numerous logs and a large cairn mark this spot for your descent route (Waypoint 2).

A path heads east (right) toward the west side of Mummy Mountain. In 25 yards, the path temporarily disappears and you scramble up a low-angled rock face. Follow the path and cairns as you continue east toward Mummy Mountain. The path becomes easy to follow as it climbs up a slope. At the top of the slope, the path again disappears. Head ENE about 30 yards and you'll pick up the path (Waypoint 3: Trail Resumes). Head north on the path about 300 yards to the chute in Photo 2. Climb the chute and head east about 100 yards to the high point on Mummy Mountain (Waypoint 4: Mummy).

Congratulations. You made it to the second highest peak in Mt. Charleston. Look for an army box containing a register at the peak. A three-foot-high shelter made out of logs lies about 60 yards to the west of the high point. This is a perfect place to escape the wind and have lunch. To the SW towers Charleston Peak; to the SE stands Griffith Peak and Red Rock Canyon; a little farther to the east is Las Vegas and Lake Mead.

PHOTO 2

To Descend: Retrace your steps by hiking to the chute. It lies 40 yards west of a shelter made out of logs. Follow the path down the class 2 chute. At the bottom of the chute, go south (left) onto the well-defined path. It parallels Mummy Mountain until it turns SW toward the ridgeline. Once on the ridgeline, the path heads west and descends about 70 yards down the north (right) side of the ridgeline. This is where people lose the path. Look for cairns. Follow the path down to where it goes across limestone. Climb down the far side of the limestone (class 1 or 2). The path resumes and heads west along the ridgeline. At the logs and cairn, follow the path south (left) down the scree slope to the North Loop Trail. Be careful on the scree slope. Go east (left) onto the North Loop Trail and follow it back to Trail Canyon. Take Trail Canyon two miles to the trailhead.

WAYPOINTS:
1. 36.29469N / 115.65605W
2. 36.29586N / 115.65702W
3. 36.29663N / 115.65063W
4. 36.29933N / 115.64954W

Introduction to Lake Mead

Lake Mead National Recreation Area (LMNRA) encompasses 1.5 million acres, which makes it twice the size of Rhode Island. The lake caters to boaters, swimmers, sunbathers, fishermen, divers, and visitors taking a tour of the Hoover Dam, a must-see attraction. The surrounding desert provides hikers with a lifetime of exploring. This seemingly barren desert has many treasures waiting for hikers to discover.

Anniversary Narrows is one of the premier family hikes in the Southwest. Millions of years of wind and water have created a 100-foot-high slot through the mountain. Don't forget your camera.

The hot water in the several hot springs found on the Gold Strike Hot Springs hike will soothe sore muscles. The pools vary and some might be dry, but there are always a few pools waiting for hikers to relax in.

The Fortress Butte/Arizona Hot Springs hike is in Arizona. The hike travels to a seemingly impossible-to-climb butte before continuing to the hot springs. Due to poor rock quality, use extreme caution while rock scrambling in LMNRA.

LMNRA is managed by the National Park Service. Permits aren't required for hiking and there are no restricted hours; however, the hike to Anniversary Narrows does have a $5 entrance fee per car. National Park Passes are accepted. The Alan Bible Visitor Center (4 miles northeast of Boulder City on US93 at NV166) is open from 8:30 a.m. to 4:30 p.m. daily. Lake Mead is on Pacific Time.

Tips: Do not wear hiking shoes with Stealth Rubber. They are not needed and the terrain will ruin the soles much faster than sandstone.

Make sure to drive the speed limit on Northshore Road, the road to Anniversary Narrows trailhead. I have always seen rangers on this road.

PHOTO 1

Anniversary Narrows
Route

Trailhead: Along Callville Wash North Road, not marked
Distance: 2 mile walk/5 mile drive (up and back via the gravel road)
Elevation gain: 200 feet
Elevation of peak: None
Time: 1–3 hours, up and back, plus exploring time
Difficulty: 1
Danger level: 1
Class: 2 (one short climb)
How easy to follow: 1
Children: Yes
Waypoints (WGS 84): See page 97
Fees: Lake Mead Pass or $5 per car; $20 annually. Golden Eagle accepted
Best season: Later Autumn, winter, and early spring

Driving Directions

From the Mirage on Las Vegas Boulevard (the Strip), go north and turn left (west) onto Sahara. In less than one mile, turn right (north) onto I-15. Take I-15 4 miles to Lake Mead. Turn right (east) onto Lake Mead. Drive 17.2 miles on Lake Mead until it dead ends into Northshore Road. Go left, drive 12.7 miles to mile mark 16, and make a left onto the signed Callville Wash North Road (94). Drive 0.2 of a mile and park where the road divides if you don't have a high-clearance vehicle (Waypoint 1). Take gravel road 94A (which veers northwest, left) and follow it about 1.3 miles (staying out of washes) to an unsigned parking area. This is just before the road descends into Lovell Wash. *Do not drive down into Lovell Wash!*

Comments: The Narrows is something that has to be seen. Cutting almost 200 yards straight through a 100-foot-high mountain, it's a miracle of nature. The hike also passes by the remnants of Anniversary Mine. You can follow an old ore track through two tunnels, which was active during the 1920s. You have the options of hiking or driving the gravel road.

Lodging: Numerous hotels in Las Vegas.

The Hike: From where you parked, if you drove on 94A, follow the road less than 100 yards into Lovell Wash. Head north (right) into the wash (Waypoint 2). The wind and rain have created fantastic sculptures into the sides of the wash. As the wash curves to the left, you can see remnants of Anniversary Mine (1922-1928) on the right bank. A side journey up along the right side of the wash follows an old ore car track through two short tunnels (see Photo1). Once past the tunnels, follow the path 30 yards as it bends to the right and drops back into the wash.

PHOTO 2

About 100 yards beyond the tunnels, the wash narrows and you enter the locally named "Anniversary Narrows" section of the wash; see Photo 2 (Waypoint 3). It's unbelievable that wind and rain created the Narrows. At times the walls are only five feet wide, but tower 100 feet above. This is a special place. Recently, rock fall has created one class 2 climb (see Photo 3). Children can be easily lifted over the boulders. Af-

PHOTO 3

ter 150 yards, the walls recede and the wash widens again. Photo 4 was taken inside the narrows.

To Return: Retrace your steps through the narrows and into the wash. Follow the wash past the mine. The road you take back to your car lies about 200 yards from the mine. It will be on the left side of the wash. Another road, on the right side of the wash, comes in just before the road on the left. It's another landmark to look for. Turn left and walk up the road to your car.

PHOTO 4

WAYPOINT (WGS 84):
1. 36.196814N / 114.687386W
2. 36.213495N / 114.706638W
3. 36.220635N / 114.702806W

PHOTO 1

Gold Strike Canyon Hot Springs
Route

Trailhead: End of road 75 A, not marked
Distance: 5 miles up and back
Elevation gain: 800 feet during the hike out
Elevation of peak: none
Time: 2.5 hours, up and back (plus time spent at the hot springs)
Difficulty: 2
Danger level: 3
Class: 3
How easy to follow: 2
Children: No
Waypoints (WGS 84): Not needed
Fees: None
Best season: Winter

Driving Directions

From Boulder City, NV, make a left at the second stop light onto US93 South (also called the 93 truck route). Drive 5.3 miles, passing the Hacienda Casino, and turn right onto an unmarked and easily missed gravel road. Drive 0.1 of a mile and turn left on road 75A. Drive 0.3 of a mile to the trailhead. A passenger car can drive to the trailhead. Photo 1 is the trailhead.

Comments: This is a visually stunning hike. The wash travels between deep canyon walls and weaves through waterfalls. The rocks and boulders can be slippery. Although it's possible to hike all the way to the Colorado River, this route description stops at the main hot springs.

There's no way to get lost once in the wash and there are many ways down the dry and wet falls. Faint green arrows painted on rocks mark the route.

Tip: If you're planning on soaking in the hot springs, wear you swim suit underneath your hiking clothes. There's no privacy at the hot springs.

Lodging: Various hotels in Las Vegas, Henderson, and Boulder City.

The Hike: From the trailhead, the wash heads east with a gentle decline. Soon you're walking between 100-foot-high canyon walls with incredible rock formations around every turn. You'll eventually come to the first dry falls. Follow the path that goes to the left. It drops back into the wash once past the falls.

Photo 2 shows the only tricky dry fall. Use the steps that have been chiseled into the boulder to aid your descent. The boulder is slippery—take it slow. There might be a rope to assist in the descent.

About 70 yards past the dry fall, you pass under electrical wires. Just beyond the electrical wires, the canyon forks; stay in the main canyon and continue in the wash. Soon you'll start to see water in the wash. Continue hiking in the wash, following the green arrows around the boulders and dry falls. In less than a half-mile you come to the hot springs (see Photo 3).

The water is very warm, perfect for soothing sore muscles. Even when the temperature in the early parts of the canyon is cold, the hot springs warm the air around it. The large hot springs can hold 25 people or more and is

PHOTO 2

about eight feet deep in parts. You can continue hiking down to the Colorado River, but the best hot springs is the one in Photo 3.

PHOTO 3

To Return: Retrace your steps. If your boots are wet, be careful of slipping. Make sure to veer to the right when passing under the power lines. If in doubt, just follow the numerous footprints.

Note: The hot springs change from year to year due to flooding and droughts. If the hot springs in Photo 3 is not full of water, continue down the canyon a short distance where you'll find more hot springs.

PHOTO 1

Fortress Butte and Arizona Hot Springs
Route

Trailhead: Dirt parking lot off US93, marked
Distance: 4 miles; 5.5 if hiking to the hot springs, up and back
Elevation gain: 900 feet
Elevation of peak: 1,884 feet
Time: 3 hours, up and back
Difficulty: 2
Danger level: 4
Class: 3
How easy to follow: 2
Children: No
Waypoints (WGS 84): See page 106
Fees: None
Best season: Winter

Driving Directions From Boulder City, NV, make a left at the second stop light onto US93 South (also called the truck route) and drive 3.9 miles past the "Welcome to Arizona" sign at Hoover Dam to a gravel road just past a bridge. Turn right and follow the gravel road 50 yards to the parking area.

Note: This will change once the Hoover Damn Overpass is completed. The completion date has only been delayed three years now, but it's on schedule to open in late 2010.

Comments: The top of the butte is larger than a football field with great views in every direction. After summiting, you have the option of hiking to the hot springs in less than one mile. Fortress Butte is visible from the trailhead (see Photo 1).

Warning: An amoeba common to thermal pools (hot springs) may be present and could enter through your nose causing a rare infection. Do not dive into the hot springs or submerge your head.

Lodging: Various hotels in Las Vegas or Henderson.

The Hike: The trail begins at the sign that reads "Lake Mead National Recreation Area White Rock Canyon–Lake Mojave (Colorado River) 2.3 miles, Arizona Hot Springs 2.8 miles." Follow the trail as it heads SW toward the Colorado River. In 100 yards the trail divides; take the left fork. Follow the trail down and across a small wash and continue onto the single-track trail. When the trail widens, veer left to find the continuation of the single-track trail. Soon you come to a divide (Waypoint 1); veer right along a faint trail. It soon becomes obvious again. As you come to a rise, the peak comes back into view (see Photo 2).

FORTRESS BUTTE

PHOTO 2

Follow the trail down into a drainage. The trail almost immediately leaves the drainage and parallels it along the left side. Leave the trail near the craggy pinnacle in Photo 3 and walk about 75 yards to a small saddle (Waypoint 2). Descend a small drainage into a wide wash. Head west (right) in the wash about 70 yards to an intersection with another wash.

Go south (left) in the new wash and hike about 200 yards. Photo 4 shows the two routes. Route A has the exposed climb; Route B avoids the climb. Both routes meet up just after the exposed climb.

Route A: Head up the loose slope in a drainage, veering left to the far end of the milkshake-colored rock (Waypoint 3). Head right walking

PHOTO 3

ROUTE A

CLIMB

ROUTE B

PHOTO 4

along the base of a 50-foot wall. The footing becomes better as you approach the climb (class 3; lots of exposure). Climb the exposed rock onto a ledge. You'll see a large cairn to your right; this marks the descent route.

Route B: Head up the loose slope in a drainage veering to the far right side of the milkshake-colored rock. Ascend a class 2 chute, passing a large cairn. The two routes merge here.

To the Summit: Continue up easy rock and veer left at the large wall ahead. Work your way up the face via cairned chutes and a bighorn sheep path. Climbing is easy class 3 or less. Once up, there's a large cairn marking the descent (Waypoint 4). Walk south a few hundred yards to the summit (Waypoint 5). There's a register to sign and incredible vistas in every direction. Walk the perimeter of the butte; you'll get an appreciation of the forces it took to create this island in the sky.

To Descend: Retrace your steps. Once past the large cairn just above the exposed climb, drop NW into the wide wash. From here you can retrace your steps to the trailhead or hike SW in the wash a little less than a mile to Arizona Hot Springs. Just stay in the wash. It ends at the hot springs. This is known as the backway to the hot springs and the way many hike back to the trailhead after soaking in the springs.

WAYPOINTS:
1. 35.97206 N / 114.70647 W
2. 35.96743 N / 114.71074 W
3. 35.96064 N / 114.71220 W
4. 35.96060 N / 114.71295 W
5. 35.95956 N / 114.71231 W

ARIZONA

Introduction to Arizona

Arizona offers a fantastic diversity of hiking. From the Grand Canyon to a 12,633-foot peak and the crystal-clear blue waters in Havasu Canyon, Arizona is an incredible place to hike. I've included three of the best hikes Arizona has to offer. Don't plan on doing all these hikes in one trip, since they're not close to one another.

When people think of Arizona, they think Grand Canyon. This book has the classic Rim to Rim to Rim hike. If you want to really see the Grand Canyon, this hike won't disappoint. It's a two-day trek, but don't worry, I've included all the information you need. The Grand Canyon is managed by the National Park Service. Permits aren't required for hiking; however, there's a $25 per vehicle entrance fee, good for seven days. All National Park passes are accepted. There are no restricted hours for hiking the trails. The Canyon View Information Plaza, located a quarter-mile from Mather Point, is open from 8 a.m. to 8 p.m. A free shuttle stops at the plaza.

Although most hikers don't realize it, Havasu Canyon is part of the Grand Canyon. The backpack to Havasupai campground and the hike to the Colorado River just might become your favorite hike in this book! When you get your first glimpse of Havasu Falls, you'll think it's a Hollywood movie set. It just doesn't look real. If you only do one backpacking hike in this book, do this one. Please check online for the current fees and permits. They change constantly.

This book wouldn't be complete without words. It also wouldn't be complete without the highest peak in Arizona. Humphreys Peak soars 12,633 feet above sea level and has magnificent views. No fees or permits are required.

All of Arizona is on Mountain Time and doesn't fall back or spring forward to account for Daylight Savings Time.

Grand Canyon Rim to Rim in Two Days

This hike is as much about planning as it is about endurance. I've tried to provide information that allows you to make the best decisions, ensuring a good experience at this classic hike.

Warning: This hike is for advanced hikers. You're pretty much on your own in many parts of the canyon. In two days, you'll hike 45 miles and gain more than 10,000 feet in elevation. More than 250 people are rescued from the depths of the canyon each year. If you can be carried out on a pack mule, the charge is $750. If you have to be evacuated by Park Service helicopter, the charge is $2,900. This can be a very expensive hike if you're not in great shape.

Brief Overview

After lodging or camping the night before on the South Rim, you get up early, catch the shuttle to the South Kaibab trailhead, and hike 22 miles to the North Rim. The elevation gain is more than 6,000 feet. You then walk 1.5 miles to the Grand Canyon Lodge, where you eat and sleep. Getting up early the next day, you catch a shuttle to the North Kaibab trailhead and hike down to Phantom Ranch. You then take the Bright Angel Trail up to the South Rim and walk to your car. On this day you hiked

23 miles and gained more than 4,400 feet in elevation. Totals: 45.5 miles and 10,400-plus feet elevation gain in two days.

Fast Facts

Mileage: 45.5 miles
Time: 2 days
Elevation gain: 10,400+ feet
Water: Yes, drinkable; no need to filter
Best season: Early autumn
Permits: None
Fees: $25 good for 7 days (Golden Eagle and
 National Park Passes accepted)
Trails: South Kaibab, North Kaibab, and Bright Angel
Time Zone: Mountain; AZ does not observe Daylight Savings Time
Notes: The North Rim closes in October and reopens around
 April 15

Lodging South Rim

Your first decision is accommodations at the South Rim. You have two choices: Camp or stay at one of the lodges. It's easier to stay at one of the lodges *inside* Grand Canyon Village. Here's a list of lodges.

Bright Angel Lodge: 888/297-2757; $79-$174
Maswik Lodge: 888/297-2757; $90-$170
Yavapai Lodge: 888/297-2757; $107-$153

Note: Xanterra handles all reservations; hence the same phone number for all lodges. *You must make reservations well in advance.* There are other accommodations, but they're more expensive.

Camping South Rim

If you want to camp, here's the information.

Mather Campground: Mather is in Grand Canyon Village at 7,000 feet and is open year-round; $18 per night, toilets and water, no hookups; 877/444-6777; www.nps.gov/grca/planyourvisit/cg-sr.htm. Other campgrounds are too far away to be practical.

Permits (not applicable for day hikes)

A backcountry permit is required for all *overnight* camping below the rim. The majority of available permits are reserved up to four months in advance.

Costs: $10 per permit and $5 per person, per night

Obtaining a Permit: Backcountry Information Center, P.O. Box 129 Grand Canyon, AZ 86023; 928/638-7875, call 1-5 p.m. Monday through Friday; website: www.nps.gov/grca/planyourvisit/permits.htm

Hikers arriving in the park without a permit might be able to obtain a permit by waiting for a last-minute space at the Backcountry Information Center. Located in the Maswik Transportation Center, South Rim; open 8 a.m. to noon and 1-5 p.m. Guests of Phantom Ranch don't need a permit.

North Rim Information

The North Rim is less commercialized than the South Rim. It's about 1,000 feet higher than the South Rim. Since it's unlikely you'll have a car at the North Rim trailhead, plan to walk the 1.5 miles to the Grand Canyon Lodge. The five-hour drive from the South Rim to the North Rim makes leaving a car at the North Rim difficult.

Lodging North Rim

There's only one lodge on the North Rim: Grand Canyon Lodge. The rooms are small, but adequate. To make reservations, call 928/638-2611. Reservations should be made well in advance.

Note: The Grand Canyon Lodge closes in October for the winter.

Camping North Rim

Camping isn't practical. You don't want to carry a tent, sleeping bag, and other camping equipment 45 miles.

Dining North Rim

There are only two places to eat at the North Rim.

Grand Canyon Lodge Dining Room: Make reservations well in advance; 928/638-2611; moderate prices and casual dress. Open 4:45-9:45 p.m.

foreverlodging.com/foreverinfo.cfm?PropertyKey=181&Content Key=2212262

Deli in the Pines: The consensus is to eat here. It's very casual. Open 7 a.m.–9 p.m.

Gift Shop

It has a few food items, but you won't be able to buy enough food or drinks for the hike back to the South Rim. In other words, carry enough food for the hike back to the South Rim. It's located next to Grand Canyon Lodge.

The **Camping Store** does have food items, but it's more than a two-mile roundtrip. However, you could stop on your way to the Grand Canyon Lodge at the end of the first day. It adds an extra quarter-mile or so. Hours: 7 a.m.-9 p.m.

Weather

With a 6,000-foot elevation change, hikers will face either hot or cold conditions. Layering is the only way to keep comfortable while hiking Rim to Rim to Rim. It could be below freezing at the trailheads. During summer months, temperatures at Phantom Ranch exceed 100 degrees. For that reason, you shouldn't attempt the hike during the summer months. Early spring finds ice and snow near the rim, making the hike impractical due to the weight of crampons you'll have to carry once the trail is free of snow and ice. This leaves early autumn as the best time to attempt the hike.

What to Bring

Flashlight or Headlamp: Most hikers start before sunrise.

Blister Kit: Just about everyone gets blisters. Moleskin, Spyroflex, duct tape, and a needle are the main components.

ID: Needed to check into lodges.

Food: You need food for both hikes and breakfast the second day. From my personal experience, the first day's hike is very deceptive, which leads to not eating enough. The first 19 miles are easy. Couple that with high temperatures and you don't feel like eating. The last few miles are strenuous. If you haven't eaten enough, it's too late. Eat! This is the best tip I can give you.

Water: Most hikers use a hydration system. Although there's drinkable water along much of the hike, you'll need to start with water. Remember, drink before you become thirsty.

Sports Drink: Start with a 32-ounce bottle of Gatorade, etc. Buy Gatorade powder and fill baggies with Gatorade powder. After you finish your original bottle of Gatorade, keep the bottle. When you come to drinkable water, fill the empty bottle with the Gatorade powder and add water. This way you'll have Gatorade throughout both days.

Daypack: There are several on the market. Remember to pack light. Since it's all trail, you can attach additional clothing to the outside of the pack.

Clothing: One word: layers. With 30- to 40-degree temperature changes, you have to wear layers. If it's hot, a cotton T-shirt will help keep you cool at the bottom of the canyon. You'll need clothes for both hikes and something to wear between hikes. *Tip: Wear old hiking clothes the first day. When you get to the North Rim, throw them away. It's less weight to carry the next day.*

Sunglasses: Protect your eyes from the bright sun.

Sunscreen: Protect your skin from the sun. Apply often.

Hat: Keeps you cool and protects you from the sun. Also, if it's cold, a hat helps keep you warm. You lose up to 80% of body heat through your head.

Boots: This is not the hike to try out new boots! Since the hike is all trail, you don't need Stealth rubber shoes. Remember the adage: A pound on the feet is like five pounds on the back. The most important thing is comfortable boots.

Hiking Socks: The best you can afford. Bring at least two pairs. Your feet get you from Rim to Rim. Treat them nicely.

Sock Liners (optional): If you use them, wear them. If you haven't used them before, this isn't the hike to see if you like them. Bring at least two pair.

Money/Credit Card: The amount depends on your spending habits.

Tevas (optional): By crossing a stream, you avoid climbing a hill. At times, there's too much water to safely cross the stream. But even when the water is low, you'll still get your boots very wet.

Toiletries: Toothbrush, deodorant, etc.

Express Hiker's Shuttle (South Rim)

Departs from: Bright Angel Lodge and Backcountry Information Center.

Destination: South Kaibab trailhead, the starting point for this hike.

Cost: None

Hours: September: 5, 6, and 7 a.m.; October: 6, 7, and 8 a.m.

Rim to Rim Shuttle

If you can't hike back to the South Rim, there's a shuttle bus that travels to the South Rim.

Cost: $80 per person

Reservations: 928/638-2820

Driving Time: About 5 hours

Mileage Charts

Day 1

South Kaibab Trailhead to:

Cedar Ridge	1.5 miles
Ribbon Falls	5.8 miles
Tonto Trail	4.4 miles
Cottonwood Camp	7.3 miles
Colorado River	6.0 miles
Roaring Springs	9.5 miles
Phantom Ranch	7.8 miles
N. Kaibab Trailhead	14.2 miles

Day 2

N. Kaibab to:

Roaring Springs	4.7 miles
Colorado River	2.1 miles
Cottonwood Camp	6.9 miles
Indian Gardens	5.2 miles
Ribbon Falls	8.4 miles
Phantom Ranch	14.2 miles
Bright Angel TH	9.8 miles

PHOTO 1

South Rim to North Rim
Trail

Day 1
Trailhead: South Kaibab also known as Yaki Point, marked
Distance: 22 miles+ 1.5 miles to Grand Canyon Lodge
Elevation gain: 6,000 feet
Time: 8-11 hours
Difficulty: 5
Danger level: 3 (dehydration)
Class: 1
How easy to follow: 1
Children: No
Waypoints: Not needed
Fees: Grand Canyon Pass $25 per car, good for 7 days;
    Golden Eagle and National Park Pass accepted
Best season: Early autumn

Driving Directions

From the town of Williams, AZ, take I-40 east two miles to Exit 165. Go north (left) on AZ64 North 62 miles to the South Entrance Road of the Grand Canyon.

Comments: Anyone who loves hiking should do this classic hike at least once. The Grand Canyon is so large you really can't comprehend it. The mighty Colorado River flows through the base of the canyon. The legendary Phantom Ranch is unique. Mules transport all supplies to the ranch. There are no roads and no cars!

How to Get to the Trailhead: From your lodge, drive east to the Backcountry Information Center. Take the Express Shuttle bus to the South Kaibab Trail. The Express and regular shuttles are free!

Note: Cars are not allowed to drive to or park at the South Kaibab trailhead.

When you finish the hike at Bright Angel trailhead (Day 2), you're only a five-minute walk from the Backcountry Information Center.

Water: None along South Kaibab Trail. Lots of *drinkable* water along the river and along North Kaibab Trail. (You do *not* need a water filter.)

The Hike: From the trailhead, you get an immediate view of the canyon. The South Kaibab Trail descends rapidly using switchbacks. In fact, this is the steepest part of the trail. At 1.5 miles, you come to Cedar Ridge. There are bathrooms, but no water. The trail continues to Skeleton Point, an overlook area only. Just beyond Skeleton Point you get your first view of the Colorado River (see Photo 1).

The trail descends quickly, then levels before coming to the junction of Tonto Trail, 4.4 miles from the trailhead. Bathrooms are located near the junction. No water here, but an emergency phone is located along the trail a few yards past the junction.

You get another view of the Colorado River soon after leaving the junction. The grade along the trail here is slight. You'll soon get your first view of the Kaibab Suspension Bridge, the bridge you take across the Colorado River (see Photo 2).

PHOTO 2

Keep an eye out for an unmarked overlook off to the left of the trail. A short path leads to the overlook. This is the first really good view of the Colorado River. Continue on the main trail to a sign indicating to go right as the trail divides. As this point the tunnel and Kaibab Suspension Bridge are a short distance away. Hike through the tunnel and across the 440-foot long bridge.

Wonder how the bridge was built? In 1928, 42 Havasupai Indians carried cables for the South Kaibab suspension bridge down the South Kaibab Trail on their shoulders. Kind of puts things in perspective!

You've hiked 6 miles and descended 4,800 feet to the bottom of the Grand Canyon. The elevation is 2,400 feet. Unless you're extremely lucky, sometime during your descent you'll run into a mule train. The mules carry people and supplies to and from Phantom Ranch. You must step aside and let the mules pass.

PHOTO 3

Follow the trail west along the Colorado River. It's very scenic and the sound of the river makes this one of the best parts of the trail. You'll soon come to the trail sign in Photo 3. If you need to make a pit stop or water, go south (left) across the bridge to the bathrooms. If not, head north (straight) paralleling Bright Angel Creek for about a third of a mile to Phantom Ranch.

You pass Bright Angel Campground and a ranger station before arriving at Phantom Ranch. The ranch is a popular stopping place for hikers, backpackers, and mule riders. Water, food, and bathrooms are available.

The cabins are reasonable, but getting a reservation is not. Try to book at least one year in advance. The ranch was designed by Mary Colter and built in 1922.

From Phantom Ranch, continue NE on the trail. Bright Angel Creek is to your left. You'll soon come to a trail sign that reads, "Ribbon Falls: 5.7; Cottonwood (Camp) 7.4; North Rim: 13.4." This part of the trail is in the shade early in the morning. About 1.2 miles from Phantom Ranch, you cross a metal bridge. In another 0.2 of a mile you cross another metal bridge. The trail has a slight incline as it crosses the third bridge since Phantom Ranch. In about 250 yards you cross the fourth bridge. Soon the canyon opens and you'll come to a place where water saturates the trail. It's easily navigated. The trail again crosses a wet area as it makes it way to Ribbon Falls. Unfortunately, you'll be in the sun regardless what time of the day you're walking this part of the trail. When you come to the Ribbon Falls Trail sign, continue straight, even if you want to go to Ribbon Falls. This trail to Ribbon Falls does *not* have a bridge. You'll get your boots wet while crossing the creek. The main trail ascends and descends a steep hill and you come to another trail sign for Ribbon Falls. Go left across a *bridge* to Ribbon Falls or go right and continue toward Cottonwood Camp. Ribbon Falls is at least a 30-minute detour. You've hiked 5.6 miles from Phantom Ranch.

PHOTO 4

As you continue to Cottonwood Camp (2.2 miles), you pass a trail sign for and cross Wall Creek almost two miles from Ribbon Falls (see

Photo 4). In less than a half-mile from Wall Creek, you come to Cottonwood Camp. There's drinking water, bathrooms, and a ranger station here. As you leave Cottonwood Camp, the trail climbs before leveling off. About one mile from Cottonwood, you pass a small waterfall. A few hundred yards beyond the waterfall, you cross a bridge and come to a house—yes, a house! An artist has lived here for years. You can get drinking water from the hose. From the house, the trail climbs via switchbacks out of the bottom of the canyon. Leaving the creek, the trail climbs and passes to the west of Roaring Spring Waterfall, the source of all water used in the Grand Canyon. You've hiked 9.3 miles from Phantom Ranch. You have another 4.7 miles to go.

The trail continues its ascent to the North Rim trailhead and weaves along the canyon wall. Looking back down into the canyon, the artist's house is still visible. The trail descends to a bridge. Beyond the bridge, the trail starts its final ascent to the North Rim. When you reach Supai Tunnel, you're two miles from the North Rim trailhead. This final rest stop has drinking water and bathrooms. Now the incline really picks up. A half-mile from Supai Tunnel, you come to the signed Coconino Overlook. Continue another 1.5 miles (it will feel longer), to the North Rim trailhead (see Photo 5). Unless you have a car at the North Rim trailhead, you have to walk to the lodge. There's no shuttle from the trailhead to the lodge.

Begin by following the trail to the campground. When the trail divides at the top of the hill, go left and cross the road. Continue past the sign that reads: Campground 0.3; Lodge 1.2 miles. Follow the trail until it

PHOTO 5

merges with the road and continue to Grand Canyon Lodge.

Make sure to sign up for the shuttle at the lodge. It's very informal. Don't expect a limousine. Hey, it beats walking 1.5 miles to the trailhead. The good news is tomorrow's hike is easier.

PHOTO 1

North Rim to South Rim
Trail

Day 2
Trailhead: North Kaibab Trail also known as North Rim, marked
Distance: 23.8 miles
Elevation gain: 4,460 feet
Time: 8-11 hours
Difficulty: 5
Danger level: 3 (dehydration)
Class: 1
How easy to follow: 1
Children: No
Waypoints: Not needed
Fees: Grand Canyon Pass $25 per car, good for 7 days;
Golden Eagle and National Park Pass accepted
Best season: Early autumn. Snow in winter; 110° in the summer.

Driving Directions

Getting to the trailhead: Make sure you made arrangements the previous day for a shuttle to take you to the trailhead. You are starting on the same trail you finished on the day before.

The Hike: The sandy trail is easy on the knees as it descends toward the bottom of the canyon. In 1.5 miles you pass the signed

Coconino Overlook. Continue another 0.5 of a mile to Supai Tunnel. Bathrooms and drinkable water are available. Continue down the trail and cross the bridge. Once across, the trail ascends slightly before descending past Roaring Springs. You've hiked 4.7 miles. Phantom Ranch is another 9.3 miles. Continue to the Artist House, where you can get water. Follow the trail across the bridge. When you pass a small waterfall, you're about one mile from Cottonwood Camp. There's drinkable water, bathrooms, and a ranger station at Cottonwood. You've hiked 6.9 miles.

In the first half-mile from Cottonwood, you come to Wall Creek. Two miles farther on the trail, you reach the cutoff for Ribbon Falls. If you didn't go there yesterday, it's worth the trip. Go right at the sign for Ribbon Falls, cross the bridge, and follow a path about a half-mile to the falls. See Photo 1. If the river is *low*, instead of backtracking to the bridge, follow the path and go right (south) at the divide. Follow the path to the creek. Put on your Tevas if you have them; if not, you'll get your boots wet. Pho-

PHOTO 2

to 2 shows the creek crossing. Look for a cairn about 25 yards south of the crossing and pick up a path that leads to the North Kaibab Trail. This shortcut saves time and distance.

When you come to a wet area on the trail, go right, following a path around the water. Once the use path disappears, head left to the main trail. Now the canyon starts to narrow. The earlier you go through the narrow part of the canyon, the shadier it will be. You'll cross four bridges in the narrows. Once across the fourth bridge, a trail sign indicates Bright Angel Trail in 0.8 of a mile. Go right at the trail sign for Bright Angel Trail and cross the bridge. If you're tired or hot, take a dip in Bright Angel Creek. Just to the left are bathrooms, drinking water, and a pay phone.

Follow the trail a couple hundred yards to the Silver Bridge. Once across the bridge, go west (right) as indicated by the trail sign. This is known as the River Trail. It parallels the Colorado River for 1.2 miles before it pulls away from the river, heads south, and becomes the Bright Angel Trail. You soon pass a stone hut off to the right. An emergency phone is located here. The trail heads up a canyon following Pipe Springs Creek, which you'll cross several times. There's intermittent shade along this section of the trail. The grade from the Silver Bridge to here is very slight. Look for a scenic waterfall off to the right.

The trail uses switchbacks to climb out of the canyon. Luckily, there's shade along part of this strenuous section. You'll cross Garden Creek. As the trail rounds a corner, it sounds like a freight train is coming at you. It's really a waterfall off to the right. The trail parallels the creek, then crosses it. You'll pass the junction for Tonto East Trail before coming to Indian Garden. This is a major rest stop with bathrooms, shade, and water.

From Silver Bridge to here is about four and a half miles. Bright Angel trailhead is another 4.5 miles and 3,060 feet higher. The three-mile round-trip trail to Plateau Point starts from Indian Gardens. You'll probably do that hike another day!

PHOTO 3

As you leave Indian Gardens, you pass a ranger's station. The next mile and a half of the trail is uneventful and dry. Off to the west is a formation known as the Battleship. As the trail climbs, make sure to look off to the south for a great vista of Indian Gardens and the Plateau Point Trail. You'll pass Three Mile Resthouse, which has drinkable water and a restroom. From here the trail climbs using switchbacks. There's a trail sign at the two-mile point. At 1.5 miles from the top, you come to 1.5 Mile Resthouse. It also has drinkable water and bathrooms. The trail becomes steeper for the next mile. You'll pass hikers descending from the top of the trail. At less than a half-mile from the top, you can see Kolb Studio, which stands at the trailhead (see Photo 3). Follow the trail to the top. Congratulations, you did it!

If hikers in your group become separated, you should meet at a pre-arranged spot at the trailhead. It's crowded and the area is quite large. Kolb Studio, which has lots of books and a gallery downstairs, is a good meeting place. It's less than a five-minute walk from Kolb Studio to the Backcountry Information Center, where you left your car.

Humphreys Peak
Trail

Trailhead: Snow Bowl, marked
Distance: 9.6 miles, up and back
Elevation gain: 3,833 feet
Elevation of peak: 12,633 feet
Time: 5-7 hours, up and back
Difficulty: 4
Danger level: 4
How easy to follow: 2
Children: No
Waypoints: Not needed
Fees: None
Best season: Summer to early autumn

Driving Directions From Flagstaff, AZ, take AZ180 west approximately seven miles to the signed Snow Bowl Ski area. Turn right and drive 7.4 miles and turn left into the signed parking area for Humphreys Peak. The signed trailhead is at the far end of the parking lot.

Comments: Humphreys Peak is the highest peak in Arizona. From the summit you can see the Grand Canyon, Sedona, and numerous peaks around Flagstaff. It's a very popular hike. *During summer months violent* *thunderstorms are frequent.* Get a very early start and be off the peak well before noon. It's normally very windy along the ridge and at the peak. Bring a windbreaker. There are bathrooms and trash containers at the trailhead.

Dogs are allowed on the trail if on a leash.

Lodging: Campgrounds starting at $15 per night.

www.flagstaffwebcam.com/Camping-And-RV

Various motels in Flagstaff, AZ.

hotel-guides.us/arizona/flagstaff-az-hotels.html

The Hike: The trail cuts across a meadow going under chair lifts. Agassiz Peak towers to the east (right). As the trail enters a thick forest, a sign indicates you're entering the Kachina Peaks Wilderness Area. The grade is slight as the trail ascends the slope. In a little less than a mile, the trail divides; go left as indicated by the trail sign. There's also a trail register here. The trail to the right goes to the ski lodge. Aspens, Engelmann spruce, and core-bark fir provide shade. You'll pass a couple of volcanic rock fields on the way to the peak. The trail continues with a slight incline, occasionally affording great views through the trees out to the west. After almost three miles, a sign indicates you've hiked to an elevation of 11,400 feet.

Your next destination is the 11,800-foot saddle that lies between Humphreys and Agassiz Peaks. It's a short trek to the saddle. Here, the trail divides again. Going left leads to Humphreys; going right onto the Weatherford trail leads past Agassiz Peak. Humphreys' summit ridge is visible from the saddle. From the saddle, the trail heads north along the west side of the summit ridge. Here, you'll encounter easy class 2 scrambles. The trail becomes obscured as boulders cover the terrain. Wooden poles with the word "trail" written on them help hikers stay on route. The trail resumes and becomes steep as it climbs to the summit ridge. The hike ascends a false peak before the real peak comes into view.

Once you can see the real peak, the trail levels and you have great views in all directions. The last 100 yards are steep, but with the summit sign in sight, it's a quick push to the highest point in Arizona.

Since this hike is known for wind, two rock shelters have been built to protect hikers from the icy gales. The register is on the far side of the main rock shelter. On a clear day, vistas include the Grand Canyon, Painted Desert, the red rocks of Sedona, Bill Williams Mountain, and Kendrick Mountain.

To Descend: Retrace your steps.

Introduction to Havasupai Backpack

The Havasupai hike to the Colorado River is one of the best trips in the Southwest. Great scenery, lots of water, and a relatively easy route make this trip a favorite. It begins at Hualapai Hilltop trailhead. Although most of the information in this section pertains to backpacking, you can ride a mule or take a helicopter down to the campground. Havasupai campground can be crowded during the peak seasons (spring and fall). If you go during summer, you will not need a tent, warm clothes, or even a sleeping bag if you really want to go light.

Tip: Slow down when driving through Peach Springs, AZ. It's a speed trap!

Brief Overview

Day 1—Backpack from Hualapai Hilltop trailhead down to the campground (10 miles).

Day 2—Hike 14 miles (round trip) to the Colorado River.

Day 3—Short optional hike into a side canyon. Backpack out to the trailhead (10 miles).

Fast Facts

Mileage: 20-mile backpack (14-mile day hike)
Time: 3 days
Elevation Lost: 2,200 feet
Water: Drinkable at campsite
Best season: Spring and Fall
Permits: $17 per night for camping
Trailhead: Hualapai Hilltop
Fees: Required to enter, $35 per person.
Time Zone: Mountain Time
Dogs: Not allowed
Closest Town: Peach Springs, gas and groceries available.
Contact Information: Havasupai Tourist Enterprise; 928/448-2121
Emergencies: The Havasupai Indians patrol the campground.

Permits

Get permits by calling Havasupai Tourist Enterprise Office at 928/448-2121 or 928/448-2141 or 928/448-2174. They can be extremely busy; keep trying. Permits can be reserved up to six months in advance and are $17 per night per person. There's an entrance fee of $35 per person and an Environmental Care Fee of $5 per person. This land belongs to the Havasupai Indians. You must pick up your permits *between 7 a.m. and 5 p.m.* at the Tourist Enterprise Office in the village. You'll be hiking right past the office. They accept credit card or cash. www.havasupaitribe.com/reservations.html. These fees change every year!

Supply Store

After hiking eight miles, you come to the village where the Supai Indians live. A store sells cold drinks, beef jerky, and other items. It's similar to a 7-Eleven. It *doesn't* have backpacking supplies. There's also a small restaurant across from the supply store. Hours: 6 a.m. to 6 p.m.

Motels

Hualapai Lodge in Peach Springs is around 65 miles from the trailhead. It has lots of amenities and offers whitewater adventures, helicopter rides, and bus tours.

Rates: Around $100 per night.

Reservations: 888/255-9550

The Lodge is located in the village. It has 24 rooms. There are no TVs or phones in the rooms.

Rates: Around $145 per night, up to four people.

Reservations: Call 928/448-2111 or 928/448-2201 or email: lodge@havasupaitribe.com.

Other Ways to the Campground

If you don't want to backpack down to the campground, you have a few alternatives.

Helicopter: $85 (one way) includes one backpack. There's a trailer in the parking lot where you pay and wait for the helicopter. It flies all day long, but the Indians get on before anyone else. You might have to wait for a long time. Once aboard, it's less than 10 minutes to the village. You backpack the two miles down to the campground.

Helicopter and Mule: $135.25 (one-way). Same as above, only a mule takes your backpack from the village to the campground. You walk to the campground.

Mule: $93.50 (one way). A mule carries your backpack to the campground. Most walk with a daypack down to the campground. You can ride a horse, but it's very dusty along the trail. Mules will carry up to four articles not weighing more than 130 pounds total. Duffel bags are highly recommended.

For more information: 928/448-2121 or www.havasupaitribe.com/horses.html

Weather Forecast (for Peach Springs, AZ)

www.weather.com/outlook/recreation/outdoors/local/USAZ0160?from=search_current

Things to Watch Out For

Sand will get in your water shoes. Sock liners help prevent your feet from getting cut by the sand. Rattlesnakes are present. Watch where you place your hands while climbing. Snakes are most active during April and October. They're usually not seen in summer—it's too hot. Scorpions crawl into things at night. Shake out shoes and clothing before you dress.

What to Bring

Blister Kit: Just about everyone gets blisters. Moleskin, Spyroflex, duct tape, and a needle are the main components of blister prevention and cure.

ID and Money: Bring money if you want to buy food and drinks at the store or restaurant.

Food: If backpacking for three days, you'll need six to seven meals, plus snacks. On Day 1, dinner (breakfast and lunch can be eaten at home or on the road); day 2, breakfast, lunch, and dinner; day 3, breakfast and lunch (dinner can be eaten on the drive home). Mountain House Freeze Dried Meals are considered the best. Walmart Supercenters have good prices, though a limited selection.

Stove and Fuel: To cook the Mountain House meals.

Matches: Waterproof are always a good choice.

Mess Kit: You can eat your meals out of the Mountain House packages. If so, all you need are a spoon and one pot to boil water.

Water: *There's no water along much of the trail to the campground.* You'll need to start with water. Remember, drink before you become thirsty. There's a spring at the campground—no need to filter. All other water must be filtered.

Water Filter: Not needed. There's drinkable water at the campground!

Sports Drink: Buy Gatorade powder and repackage in baggies. Fill an empty bottle with the powder and add water. This way you'll have Gatorade throughout the trip. Three days of nothing but water gets old.

Daypack: There are several on the market. If you do any of the day hikes, you'll want a daypack.

Clothing: Depends on the month. Keep in mind you will get wet. If hot, shorts and T-shirts will be all you need.

Camp Towel: Dry off after bathing and swimming.

Sunglasses: Protect your eyes from the bright sun.

Sunscreen: Protect your skin from the sun. Apply often.

Hat: Keeps you cool and protects you from the sun.

Boots: You'll be walking trail for 10 miles on dry land with a light load (compared to most backpacks). A lightweight hiking shoe is sufficient. Even more important is a water shoe. Teva has several models. You'll cross Havasu Creek several times on your hike to the Colorado River.

Hiking Socks: Only one pair is needed. You can wash them in the creek.

Sock Liners: Mandatory if you wear water shoes. Sock liners protect your feet from the grinding sand.

Tevas (optional): Great for around the campsite.

Toiletries: Toothbrush, deodorant etc.

Tent: Depends. If it's warm, you don't need it.

Sleeping bag or Bivvy sack: You might go without in warm weather.

Thermarest: A nice luxury.

Hiking Poles: Personal preference.

Mileage Charts

Day 1

The Village:	8.0 miles
Campsite (total):	10.0 miles

Day 2

Mooney Falls:	1.0 miles
Beaver Falls:	3.0 miles
Colorado River (roundtrip):	7.0 miles

Day 3

Side Canyon (optional):	1.5 miles
The Village:	2.0 miles
Hualapai Hilltop (trailhead):	10.0 miles

PHOTO 1

Hualapai Hilltop to Campground
Trail

Day 1
Trailhead: Hualapai Hilltop, trail
Distance: 10 miles (one way)
Elevation lost: 2,200 feet
Time: 4-6 hours
Difficulty: 2
Danger level: 2 (dehydration and flash flooding)
Class: 1
How easy to follow: 2
Children: No
Waypoints: Not needed
Fees/permits: $35 entrance fee per person/$10 per person,
    per night to camp
Best season: Spring and autumn (May is the best month)

Driving Directions From Peach Springs, AZ, the last place you can get gas, head east on Route 66 for 6.5 miles and turn left onto Frazier Well Supai Road. This is AZ18, but the only sign reads Frazier Well Supai. Drive 60 miles where the road ends at the parking area. There are bathrooms at the trailhead.

Comments: This is one of the best backpacking trips in the Southwest. The scenery is unbelievable. Once at the campgrounds, two of the waterfalls are less than a half-mile away. The hike to the Colorado River is one of the best hikes in the country. It's not the hike for those who are scared of water or exposure.

Note: You must yield to all pack animals.

The hike: From the trailhead, the trail descends sharply for about one mile. In another half-mile, the trail reaches the canyon bottom. From here the trail heads north. There are easily missed mileage markers along the trail. Around mile 6 the canyon divides; go left following the trail. Soon after the trail enters Havasu Canyon, Havasu Creek appears. You must filter this water.

When the trail divides, veer right and walk across the bridge. As you round the bend, two rock pinnacles appear. They stand guard over the village of Supai. Continue another 0.25 of a mile to the Tourist Office, where you pick up your permits (see Photo 1). As seen in the photo, there might be a wait.

Continue through the village, bearing right as indicated by trail signs. About 1.75 miles from the village, a sign reads: No Jumping. Walk over to the sign and look down at Havasu Falls. No photos can capture the beauty (see Photo 2). It looks unreal! Continue down the hill, through the cattle guard, and into the campground.

Note: Due to the flood in 2008, some things might have changed.

PHOTO 2

Where to Camp: The campground parallels Havasu Creek for almost a half-mile. In about 150 yards, you see a sign for drinking water. A stone and wood hut holds the purification system. This is the only drinkable water in the campground. All other water should be filtered. I'd camp on the far side of the hut to avoid the smell from the outhouses located at the entrance to the campground. The only other outhouses are at the far end of the campground. You don't want to be too far from the outhouses or drinking water. If possible, make camp near the left wall of the canyon. You will have plenty of shade here. These campsites go fast. For more privacy you can camp on the other side of the creek, but crossing the creek is not convenient.

PHOTO 1

Hike to the Colorado River
Route

Day 2
Trailhead: Havasu Campground, marked
Distance: 14 miles, up and back
Elevation lost: 800 feet
Time: 7-10 hours, up and back
Difficulty: 3
Danger level: 4 (exposure and flash flooding)
Class: 5, fixed rope or ladder at class 5 section
How easy to follow: 4
Children: No
Waypoints: Not needed
Fees: None if paid $35 entrance fee to enter reservation
Permits: None
Best season: Spring and autumn (May is the best month)

Comments: This is one of the best hikes in the Southwest. Unbelievable scenery, great waterfalls, and lots of swimming holes make this a hike of a lifetime. If you take a camera, you should have a dry bag. Although the trail is overrun by vegetation in a few sections, shorts are recommended if it's warm. I wore shorts and didn't get scratched. None of the creek crossings were slippery, but some of the boulders were (sand).

Do not attempt this hike if the creek is flooded. Do not try to swim in the Colorado River. You will drown.

Note: This description is only a general guide on how to hike to the Colorado River. Many paths lead to the river. Due to occasional floods, parts of the route will change. Be persistent and take your time. It's well worth it!

The Hike: From the campgrounds, follow the trail to the top of Mooney Falls. Continue down the trail to the tunnel in Photo 1. You go through this tunnel and another tunnel as you make your way down to the bottom of Mooney Falls. This is a steep descent aided with chains (see Photo 2). The rock might be wet with mist from the waterfall. Once at the base of the waterfall, the trail resumes on the same side of the creek as the descent. You cross the creek several times. The first two crossings were the deepest. We took off our packs.

PHOTO 2

Around two and half miles, the trail descends via switchbacks and you do a double creek crossing. At this point you're to the right of the creek. Shortly after the double creek crossing, climb a chute filled with dirt.

In 200 yards from the dirt chute, you descend a steep dirt chute (see Photo 3). Follow the trail, staying right of the creek, to the climb and rope in Photo 4. This is a class 5 climb—use the rope *after testing* it. There might be a ladder here.

Continue along the trail, which stays high above the creek. You soon come to a boundary sign that marks the division between Havasu Tribal land and the Grand Canyon. Beaver Falls, a great place to stop on the hike back, is visible below. The sign serves as a landmark. At this point, you

PHOTO 3

PHOTO 4

have hiked about three miles; four more miles to the Colorado River. The trail drops down to the creek via cairned class 3 ledges. Shortly you cross the creek. You're now on the left side of the creek. In the next half mile you will cross the creek several times. There are some great spots to jump into the creek … literally! (See Photo 5.)

As you continue on the trail, the canyon bends. Follow the trail through a tunnel. You soon arrive at the narrows where you literally swim to the Colorado River (see Photo 6). Most of it is wading, but you will have to swim a few yards. Leave your daypack here. Make sure to stop at the sandbar. *DO NOT swim into the Colorado River.* If you don't want to swim, you can walk along ledges above the water to the Colorado River (see Photo 6 again).

At the sandbar veer left to dry land. Climb the broken wall and veer left following a path back to the start of the narrows (see Photo 7). It's a short and scenic walk back to the

PHOTO 5

PHOTO 6

start of the narrows. There's a good chance others will be there. People rafting the Colorado River stop here.

Return Trip with Optional Stop at Beaver Falls: Unfortunately, you have to leave and hike back to the campground. Begin by making sure you have everything and retrace your steps. In about four miles you

PHOTO 7

PHOTO 8

come to the boundary sign: Grand Canyon and Havasu Tribal land. Just beyond the sign follow a steep path down toward the river and Beaver Falls (see Photo 8).

After relaxing at Beaver Falls, retrace your steps back to the main trail and follow it about three miles back to the campground.

PHOTO 1

Hualapai Hilltop

Day 3

Backpack out to Trailhead: Retrace your steps on the same trail (10 miles) to Hualapai Hilltop.

Additional Hike: Good hike to do on the final day if not leaving early: Side Canyon, route

Trailhead: Havasu Campground, marked

Distance: 3 miles, up and back

Elevation lost: 200 feet

Time: 2 hours, up and back

Difficulty: 2

Danger level: 4 (exposure and flash flooding)

Class: 4, chains to aid with descent to Mooney Falls

How easy to follow: 2

Children: No

Waypoints: Not needed

Fees: None, if paid $35 entrance fee to enter reservation

Permits: None

Best season: Spring and autumn (May is the best month)

Tips: If it's warm, consider getting an early start to beat the heat. Another plan is to wait until 3 p.m. to start. This avoids ascending the last mile, which is steep, during the heat of the day. Stop at the village and buy Gatorade and a bag of ice. Fill your bladder with ice.

Comments: This is a nice hike on your final day or on the first day. It's easy, scenic, and you should have the canyon to yourself. You don't need water shoes for this hike.

The Hike: From the campgrounds, follow the trail to the top of Mooney Falls. Continue down the trail to the tunnel (see Photo 1 in the above hike). Go through this and another tunnel as you make your way down to the bottom of Mooney Falls. This is a steep descent aided with chains (see Photo 2 in the above hike). The rock might be wet with mist from the waterfall.

Once at the base of the waterfall, the trail resumes on the same side of the creek as the descent. Follow the trail about 200 yards to an obvious side canyon to the left. Follow any of the paths (they all converge) into the canyon. Although this is a boxed-in canyon, it's nice and quiet back here (see Photo 3).

To Return: Retrace your steps back to the campground.

Introduction to Sedona, Arizona

Sedona is a small town in northcentral Arizona, a mystical place with incredible scenery, many sightseeing opportunities, and some unique hikes. Many famous artists call Sedona their home and have art galleries you can browse.

I've included three of the best hikes Sedona has to offer. Boynton Canyon is the hike with the much-talked-about vortexes, a must-do hike. Bear Mountain has fantastic views, coupled with an interesting trail, making this hike one of the best around Sedona. Wilson Mountain has great views around every twist and turn and one of the best overlooks I've ever seen!

The land around Sedona is managed by the U.S. Forest Service. Permits aren't required for hiking; however, there's a $5 parking fee per vehicle. There are no restricted hours for hiking the trails. There's no visitor center dedicated to hiking, but there's a tourist center in uptown Sedona (331 Forest Road). Hours are 8:30 a.m.-5 p.m. Monday through Saturday, 9 a.m.-3:00 p.m. on Sunday. Sedona doesn't allow clocks or watches, so who cares about the time? Seriously, Sedona, like the rest of Arizona, is on Mountain Time.

BOYTON CANYON

Boynton Canyon
Trail

Trailhead: Boynton Canyon road, marked
Distance: 6.5 miles, up and back
Elevation gain: 500 feet
Elevation of peak: none
Time: 3 hours, up and back
Difficulty: 2
Danger level: 1
How easy to follow: 1
Children: Yes
Waypoints: Not needed
Fees: $5 per day
Best season: Spring and autumn

Driving Directions

From the intersection of AZ89A and 179 in Sedona, AZ, drive 3.2 miles SW on 89A and make a right turn onto Dry Creek Road. Follow it 2.9 miles and turn left on FR152C. At 1.6 miles, you reach another junction. Turn right onto Boynton Canyon Road and drive another 0.3 of a mile to the parking lot on the right. There's additional parking along side the road. You must display a Red Rock parking pass in your vehicle.

Fee: $5 parking pass is required. They're available in numerous places in Sedona. More information: www.redrockcountry.org/passes-and-permits/where-to-purchase.shtml.

Comments: The canyon is one of four vortex areas Sedona is famous for. The scenery all along the trail is unbelievable. As a bonus you'll pass by high sandstone cliffs once inhabited by the Sinagua. Remains of their ancient dwellings are still concealed in the cliff walls; however, the Forest Service has blocked off access.

Lodging: Various hotels and motels in Sedona.
www.gatewaytosedona.com/department/category/lodging
Campgrounds: $17 to $20 per night.
www.dreamsedona.com/sedona-campgrounds.html

The Hike: The signed trail heads north and immediately passes a kiosk with a log book. The trail soon divides; take the left fork as indicated by the sign. For about a mile, the trail overlooks the Enchantment Resort as it cuts across the foothills and heads north into the canyon. Once beyond the resort, a trail sign points you to the right. The trail narrows to a single-track as it parallels a creekbed. It heads west and then bends to the SW as it travels deeper into the canyon. The terrain changes from manzanita and evergreen trees to Ponderosa pine and Douglas fir. The views are spectacular along this part of the hike. Continue to a vortex area along the right side of the trail. There are dozens of cairns. I experienced a surge of energy at this area. It felt like being charged in an electrical storm. Some hikers may choose to turn around here.

The trail continues SW as the temperature drops and the grade increases. High canyon walls surround you. As you look ahead, you can see the end of the boxed-in canyon. The trail crosses a dry creekbed and climbs a small hill. It makes a sharp right and abruptly ends at a sign. The towering wall in front of you is part of Secret Mountain. You can get an overview of the canyon you just hiked by scrambling east (right) out on the sandstone. Follow the sandstone ledge a few hundred yards till it ends. Although you could climb out of the canyon, it's not recommended.

To Descend: Retrace your steps.

Bear Mountain
Trail and Route

Trailhead: Along Boynton Canyon Road, marked
Distance: 5 miles, up and back
Elevation gain: 1,900 feet
Elevation peak: 6,506 feet
Time: 3 to 5 hours, up and back
Difficulty: 3
Danger level: 2
Class: 2
How easy to follow: 2
Children: No
Waypoints: Not needed
Fees: $5 per day
Best season: Spring and autumn

Driving Directions

From the intersection of AZ89A and 179 in Sedona, AZ, drive 3.2 miles SW on 89A and make a right turn onto Dry Creek Road. Follow it 2.9 miles and turn left on FR152C. At 1.6 miles, you reach another junction. Turn left onto Boynton Canyon road and drive another 1.1 miles to the parking lot on the left. You must display a Red Rock parking pass in your vehicle.

Fee: $5 parking pass is required. They're available in numerous places in Sedona. More information: www.redrockcountry.org/passes-and-permits/where-to-purchase.shtml.

Comments: This hike is another gem. Fantastic views, coupled with an interesting trail, make this hike one of the best around Sedona. The true summit is much farther than you think. It seems the trail keeps going and going. Don't be fooled into thinking the summit is just north of the trailhead, it isn't. There're no bathrooms at the trailhead. If hiking during the summer, get an early start. There's no shade along the trail.

Lodging: Various hotels and motels in Sedona.
www.gatewaytosedona.com/department/category/lodging
Campgrounds: $17 to $20 per night.
www.dreamsedona.com/sedona-campgrounds.html

The Hike: Head north on the trail (see Photo 1). It soon crosses two dry washes as it makes it way to the sandstone monolith. The grade increases as the trail weaves past the first cliff band. Keep an eye out for blocked trails. It appears the Forest Service has recently rerouted the trail. About halfway up a chute, the trail curves to the right. The trail temporarily levels out as it goes across the first plateau. It heads NE into a side canyon and travels behind the monolith in Photo 1.

PHOTO 2

PHOTO 3

PHOTO 4

The grade becomes strenuous before climbing onto the densely vegetated mesa. Off in the distance you can see the false summit (see Photo 2). In fact, you can see over a hundred miles on a clear day! Follow the cairns as the trail goes across a short section of sandstone. The trail continues NW and descends slightly before climbing the next hill. You have a great view into Fay Canyon off to the south (see Photo 3).

The trail levels and descends again before starting another strenuous climb. Cairns keep you on track as the trail goes up whitish sandstone. Here you'll encounter some class 2 climbing. Once past the sandstone, the grade becomes steep and the true summit comes into view (see Photo 4).

Ironically, trees obscure the view from the summit, hence you really can't tell you're at the summit. Continue on the trail a short distance to the overlook. There's no cairn or sign-in book at the overlook, but the views are magnificent. Looking north you can see the San Francisco Peaks near Flagstaff (see Photo 5).

To Descend: Retrace your steps. The views are even better during the return trip!

PHOTO 5

Wilson Mountain
Trail

Trailhead: Along Alternate US89, marked
Distance: 11.6 miles or 7.5 miles, up and back
Elevation gain: 2,562 feet
Elevation of peak: 7,122 feet
Time: 5-7 hours, up and back
Difficulty: 3
Danger level: 2
Class: 1
How easy to follow: 1
Children: No
Waypoints: Not needed
Fees: $5 per day
Best season: Spring and autumn

Driving Directions

From the intersection of AZ89A and 179 in Sedona, AZ, drive north two miles and turn left into the signed parking lot. The parking lot is just after you drive over the Midgley Bridge. You need to display the Red Rock parking pass in your vehicle.

Fee: $5 parking pass is required. You can buy the pass 24 hours a day from a vending machine at the parking lot.

Comments: This is my favorite hike in Sedona. Around every corner the views get better. The southern overlook is one of the best views I've ever seen. If you only go to the southern overlook, the round trip distance is 7.5 miles. The northern overlook offers a good vista up the canyon and in the distance you can see Humphreys Peak (12,633 feet), highest in Arizona.

Lodging: Various hotels and motels in Sedona.
www.gatewaytosedona.com/department/category/lodging
Campgrounds: $17 to $20 per night.
www.dreamsedona.com/sedona-campgrounds.html

The Hike: Make sure to head north (right) onto the trail at the sign. (The trailhead is the start to several trails.) The trail starts off at a moderate grade, but levels after 100 yards. In less than a half-mile, the views are magnificent. The trail weaves around scrub oak, manzanita, and a few pinion pines. At about a half-mile, the trail intersects with the Wilson Canyon trail; continue north (straight) as indicated by the trail sign. In a few yards you'll come to a self register. From here you can see the southern overlook on Wilson Mountain (see Photo 1).

The trail soon becomes rocky, but the view easily makes up for it. As the trail temporarily heads west you get a good view down into Wilson Canyon. In about a mile, the terrain changes to a thick grove of pinion pines and the grade increases as the trail temporarily heads east. For the next 0.75 of a mile, the trail heads north and climbs to a saddle. This is the steepest part of the hike. Near the saddle the wind picks up. If you're doing this hike during the cooler months, bring a windbreaker.

At the saddle the trail levels and heads NW through open grassland. In a couple hundred yards, the trail intersects the North Wilson trail, which starts near Oak Creek Canyon. A trail sign marks this spot. The saddle is also known as the First Bench.

The grade increases as the trail enters a forest of Ponderosa pines and Gambel oak. The trees offer much-needed shade on a warm day. The trail heads north and the grade lessens. At about 3.5 miles from the trailhead, you come to a tool shed.

The trail divides here. To the south (left) is the best overlook. It's an easy 0.25 of a mile walk along a path. The view will simply take your breath away. You can see all the way down into Sedona. If you're short on time or tired, go to the overlook, then retrace your steps back to the trailhead.

For the rest of us, go to the southern overlook and come back to the tool shed. At the tool shed head west (left) or if you didn't go to the southern overlook, continue straight (west) on the trail. You're walking on top of a huge mesa. Many of the mountains around Sedona don't have definite peaks. Continue north almost two miles across the mesa to the northern overlook. The walking here is very easy. The northern overlook offers good views of East Pockets, Vultees Arch, and Humphreys Peak. There's another good overlook less than 100 yards to the SW (left). Follow the path to this overlook. Neither overlook has a sign-in book, but the views are incredible.

To Descend: Retrace your steps.

UTAH

Introduction to Bryce Canyon

Bryce Canyon is home to some of the most magnificent scenery on the planet! From hoodoos to colored pinnacles, it's a must destination for anyone who loves the outdoors. The area offers some of the world's best air quality and has panoramic views of nearly 200 miles. It's one of America's most popular national parks. Don't forget to bring your camera.

The three hikes in this chapter are fairly easy. Queens Garden Complex and Navajo Loop are two of the best family hikes in the Southwest, with amazing scenery around every corner. Fairyland Loop is the premier hike in Bryce Canyon. You get to see all the canyon has to offer and since it begins outside of the park, you don't have to pay the entrance fee.

Bryce Canyon is managed by the National Park Service. Permits aren't required for hiking; however, there's a $25 per vehicle entrance fee, good for seven days. All National Park passes are accepted. There are no restricted hours for hiking the trails. The Visitor Center, located 1.5 miles inside of Bryce Canyon's northern boundary, is open from 8 a.m.-8 p.m. daily in the summer; 8 a.m.-6 p.m. spring and autumn, and 8 a.m.-4:30 p.m. during winter months. Bryce Canyon is on Mountain Time.

PHOTO 1

Fairyland Loop
Trail

Trailhead: Fairyland Point, marked
Distance: 8 miles, closed loop
Elevation gain: 750 feet
Elevation of peak: None
Time: 4-5 hours, up and back
Difficulty: 2
Danger level: 2
How easy to follow: 1
Class: 1
Children: No
Waypoints: Not needed
Fees: None
Best season: Spring, summer, and fall

Driving Directions

From Best Western Ruby's Inn on Utah 63, drive two miles and turn east (left) on an *unsigned* paved road. Follow it one mile to Fairyland Point, the trailhead.

Comments: This is a must-do hike. In fact, many have rated it as the best hike in the Southwest. Bryce Canyon is unbelievable and this hike is the best way to see and experience it all. You'll not be disappointed. Since the trailhead is located before the fee booth, there's no entrance fee for this hike. Luckily, this trail is much less crowded than other trails in Bryce Canyon.

Lodging: Best Western Ruby's, www.rubysinn.com.

The Hike: From the parking lot, walk past the Fairyland Canyon sign to the signed Fairyland trail (see Photo 1). Don't follow the Rim trail. The view from the trailhead is unbelievable. The trail starts with a mild descent as it heads east along a ridge. In about 250 yards, a spur path heads straight to an overlook as the trail curves to the left. If you follow the spur path, you can descend a footpath from the overlook to the trail. You don't have to retrace your steps. Surprisingly, the trail weaves between Douglas fir, juniper, and limber pine trees. Out to the east are incredible formations, including the Sinking Ship (see Photo 2).

PHOTO 2

In about a mile, the trail reaches the canyon floor and crosses a dry wash. Do not attempt this hike if it's raining—flash floods can be a real problem here. As the trail ascends, you get a view all the way across the canyon and down into a distant valley. In the next half-mile, the trail passes a couple of unsigned overlooks. From the second overlook, the trail starts to climb and you gain a view into another part of the canyon. The trail descends into the bottom of the canyon again and you'll see two trail signs. The first sign indicates Tower Bridge is 200 yards away. The second sign specifies Sunrise Point is 1.7 miles away. The signs also mark the halfway point of the hike (four miles). I recommend taking the spur path to Tower Bridge. It's a great place to eat and relax in the shade (see Photo 3).

From the Tower Bridge area, retrace your steps to the Sunrise Point sign and continue on the trail. You'll soon cross a wash three times as the trail starts a long climb to the rim. The trail levels briefly. This is one of most scenic parts of the trail. The trail climbs to a single tree (see Photo 4). You now enter a different part of the canyon. Looking west, you can see the rim and people at Sunrise Point. Looking back to the east, you can see more than 100 miles! There's no pollution around Bryce Canyon.

PHOTO 3

Just before the rim, you'll see a sign for the Rim trail. You have the options of hiking 0.2 of a mile to Sunrise Point or heading north (right) on the Rim trail to Fairyland Point (3.4 miles), the trailhead. It's worth hiking to Sunrise Point. You can't miss Sunrise Point, where there are lots of people and a large sign. Queen's Garden trail starts at Sunrise Point. From Sunrise Point retrace your steps back along the Rim trail to the intersection (0.2 of a mile) and continue north on the Rim trail. The

PHOTO 4

trail stays near the rim and offers great vistas into the canyon. As the trail ascends you pass North Campground off to the west (left). At this point, a spur trail takes off to a small arch on the rim. The trail climbs and goes through a burnt area. From here to the trailhead (about two miles), the trek is easy, but seems to go on and on. The views are sporadic and the burn area seems endless. Finally, you reach Fairyland Point, the trailhead.

PHOTO 1

Queen's Garden Complex
Trail

Trailhead: Sunrise Point, marked
Distance: 1.8 miles, up and back
Elevation gain: 320 feet
Elevation of peak: None
Time: 1 hour, up and back
Difficulty: 1
Danger level: 1
Class: 1
How easy to follow: 1
Children: Yes
Waypoints: Not needed
Fees: $25, good for seven days. Golden Eagle accepted.
Best season: Spring, summer, and fall

Driving Directions

From UT12 and UT63, turn right (south) on 63. Go south on 63 less than five miles to the fee booth at the entrance to the park. Drive south 0.4 of a mile to the signed turnoff for Sunrise Point. Turn left and drive 0.6 of a mile following signs to the parking lot. Walk south to the signed trailhead for Queen's Garden Complex (see Photo 1).

Comments: This is the easiest hike in Bryce Canyon that travels from the rim to the bottom of the canyon. As with other hikes in Bryce, the views are unbelievable.

Lodging: Best Western Ruby's Inn, www.rubysinn.com.

PHOTO 2

PHOTO 3

The Hike: From the trailhead, the trail uses switchbacks to descend a slope. Immediately, you're treated to incredible views (see Photo 2). The views include Boat Mesa, the Sinking Ship, and the Aquarius to the NE. The trail continues descending the slope until it curves south and uses a series of switchbacks to drop deeper into the canyon. Spires and hoodoos mark the landscape. At the signed junction, go right as indicated by a trail sign. In 50 yards from the junction, the trail

PHOTO 4

goes through an arch. In the next 300 yards you'll walk through two more arches (see Photo 3).

Continue straight at the next junction and walk 100 yards to the end of the trail. Going left at the junction takes you to the Navaho Loop trail. Photo 4 is the formation known as Queen Elizabeth, which stands near the termination of the trail.

To Return: Retrace your steps.

PHOTO 1

Navajo Loop—Closed Loop
Trail

Trailhead: Sunset Point, marked
Distance: 1.4 miles
Elevation gain: 521 feet
Elevation peak: None
Time: 60–90 minutes, complete loop
Difficulty: 2
Danger level: 1
Class: 1
How easy to follow: 1
Children: Yes
Waypoints: Not needed
Fees: $25, good for seven days. Golden Eagle accepted.
Best season: Spring, summer, and fall

Driving Directions

From UT12 and UT63, turn right (south) on 63. Go south on 63 less than five miles to the fee booth at the entrance to the park. Drive 1.2 miles and turn left into Sunset Point.

Comments: This must do hike passes favorite formations such as Wall Street, Twin Bridges, and Thor's Hammer. Restrooms and drinking water are available at the trailhead.

Lodging: Best Western Ruby's Inn, www.rubysinn.com.

The Hike: The paved trail starts with a safety railing along the exposed edge. After about 100 yards of switchbacks, the trail divides. Although you can take either fork, go left and continue descending the east loop of the trail. Soon you'll pass Thor's Hammer off to the left (see Photo 1).

The trail enters a narrow canyon with 100-foot ponderosas rising toward the sky. At 0.4 of a mile from the trailhead, look left for a short spur trail leading to the Two Bridges formation (see Photo 2).

The trail descends gently to the bottom of the canyon and soon forks. Going left takes you to the Queen's Garden trail. Go right and continue on the Navajo Loop trail to the intersection with the Peekaboo Loop trail. Go right to continue on the Navajo trail. Soon the trail weaves through Wall Street, a short but amazing slot canyon. Entering Wall Street, two towering Douglas firs greet you. They have been greeting hikers for more than 750 years (see Photo 3). Emerging from Wall Street, the trail ascends via steep switchbacks. Once you intersect the east loop of the trail, go left to Sunset Point, the trailhead.

PHOTO 2

PHOTO 3

Introduction to Kanab, Utah

Though Kanab is just a small town in Utah, it's home to two of the best hikes in the Southwest. Located 45 minutes from Kanab, you'll find the trailhead for the Wave and Buckskin Gulch. Although they share the same trailhead, these hikes couldn't be more different.

The Wave is a must-see attraction! It's hard to describe, though you've probably seen photos; the Wave is the lower-right image on the cover of this book. It's an easy hike, though not easy to find, and is actually quite small. Photographers from all over the world hike to the Wave for that once-in-a-lifetime photo. You won't be disappointed.

Buckskin Gulch is the longest slot canyon in the world. At times the walls are only three feet wide, yet they tower 500 feet into the air. This is one of the top five hikes in the country! You can do the hike as a backpack or a day hike. I prefer doing it as a day hike.

Since both of these hikes start at the same trailhead, you could easily do these hikes in two days. The Wave requires permits and they're not easy to get. Buckskin Gulch also requires permits, but if you're day hiking, a $6 self-issued permit is located at the trailhead. The area is managed by the BLM. There's no visitor center, but a ranger station is located between mile markers 20 and 21 on US89. It's open Monday through Friday from 8:30 a.m.-4:30 p.m. Kanab, UT, is on Mountain Time.

Buckskin Gulch/Paria Canyon
Route

Trailheads: Wildcat, start; Whitehouse, end (both are marked)
Distance: 20 miles total (one way; car shuttle required)
Elevation gain: Less than 200 feet
Time: All day
Difficulty: 3
Danger level: 5 (flash floods, cold water)
Class: 4 (one down climb)
How easy to follow: 1
Children: No
Waypoints (WGS 84): See page 180
Fees: $6 per person
Permits: Self-issued. See below.
Best season: Late spring, early autumn, very hot during the summer
Equipment: 40 feet of rope or webbing, water shoes

Driving Directions

From Kanab, UT, head east on US89 for 37 miles and turn right onto the signed House Rock Valley Road. It's between mile markers 26 and 25. It's also labeled Road 700 on some maps. After a few hundred yards, it becomes a gravel road. Drive 8 miles to the signed Wire Pass trailhead parking area. There's a pit toilet at the parking area.

Note: Your mileage might vary slightly due to tire size and air pressure.

A high-clearance vehicle is recommended, but not mandatory. The road becomes impassable after a heavy rain.

Car Shuttle: You need to leave car(s) at Whitehouse trailhead, where the hike ends. This requires a car shuttle that takes almost an hour (if done from the Wire Pass trailhead) and should be *done the night before* if possible.

Coming from Kanab, head east on US89 for 42 miles (just east of mile marker 21) and turn right onto a gravel road. (A sign indicates the visitor center.) Drive 0.1 of a mile and turn left at the sign reading: Whitehouse trailhead. Drive 2.0 miles down this well-groomed dirt/gravel road to the trailhead. A passenger car can easily make this drive unless the road is wet. There's plenty of parking for cars and there are pit toilets. Make note of what this trailhead looks like, since you'll be hiking back here after a long day.

Drive back out to US89, turn left, and drive 4.9 miles on US89 to the signed House Rock Valley Road. Turn left and follow this gravel road 8 miles, passing the Buckskin trailhead. Pull off to the Wire Pass trailhead. A passenger car can make this drive, but it's slow going.

Cautions: People have died due to flash floods while hiking Buckskin Gulch. Check with rangers at BLM Paria Ranger Station (between mile markers 20 and 21 on US89) before hiking, 435/644-4600. You'll drive past the ranger station when you leave a car(s) at Whitehouse trailhead.

Permits: Self-issued permits ($6 per person) are required for day hiking. They're located at the Wire Pass trailhead. Because these requirements change, please look at this website: www.blm.gov/az/asfo/paria/permits.htm. Bring cash!

Comments: Buckskin Gulch is the longest slot canyon in the world. At times the walls are only three feet wide, yet the tower 500 feet into the air. This is one of the top five hikes in the country! The amount of water can vary greatly in the canyon. When I was there, I lost count how many times we waded through water. The water was almost chest deep. Other times, you might only encounter knee-deep water. Either way, I recommend wearing water shoes. Bring your own water. Don't try to drink or filter the water found in Buckskin. It will clog your filter. Make sure to bring a camera.

Lodging: You need to decide where you'll sleep the night before the hike. You can stay in Kanab or car camp at the Wire Pass trailhead. *There's* *no charge and no permit is required to car camp at Wire Pass.* Unless you hate car camping, this is the way to go, versus staying in Kanab.

Car Camping at Wire Pass Trailhead: Spots are limited because of the slope of the land; however, we found a great spot for one tent across from the parking area. It's just 30 feet to the right of the trail.

The Hike: The trail starts across from the sign in register in the parking lot. It's marked only with an arrow on a two-foot wooden post. In less than 100 yards, you pass through a cattle guard. The trail soon drops into a wash. Continue in the wash, *passing* a sign for Coyote Butte (The Wave). When the wash begins to narrow and the walls heighten, scramble out of the wash to the right (marked by a cairn) and follow a path across sandstone, which soon drops back into the wash/canyon. You can stay in the wash, but we had backpacks on and the obstacles required taking them off to down climb.

Either way, continue down Wire Pass Canyon to the intersection of Buckskin Gulch (1.7 miles from the trailhead). Actually, the narrowest part of the entire hike is in Wire Pass Canyon, not Buckskin! There are quite a few petroglyphs at the junction of the two canyons (Waypoint 1). They're located on the right wall of Wire Pass just before the junction. Check the sky before entering Buckskin Gulch. There are only a few exits if a flood occurs.

Turn right into Buckskin (left takes you out to the actual Buckskin Gulch trailhead, a much longer and less interesting route) and get ready for an amazing adventure. Where you first encounter water depends when it last rained. The water is very muddy and will be cold at times. Be careful of slippery mud throughout the canyon. None of the 20+ pools we waded through had dropoffs.

When you come to a minor boulder jam, head to the right to bypass it. Continue scrambling over boulders as you make your way down the canyon. Roughly three miles from the intersection of Wire Pass and Buckskin, there's a class 4 climb out. It might not get you entirely out of the canyon, but you can climb high enough to avoid water from a flood (see Photo 1). You have to turn around to see the climb out; however, there's a great landmark. About 40 yards past the climb out, it appears the canyon ends in towering walls.

In this section if the water is deep, be prepared to carry your packs. This isn't a big deal if dayhiking, but if backpacking, it's a major nuisance. At 6.5 miles from the Wire Pass-Buckskin intersection, you come to the climb out to the Middle Trail. This is another escape route if flash flood-

PHOTO 2

ing occurs (see Photo 2). There was a cairn in front of the bush when I was there. The tipoff is that the canyon walls start to lower dramatically before reaching the climb out. There are some excellent petroglyphs just to the right of the climb out.

Just beyond the climb out to the Middle Trail, the canyon widens and sun fills the canyon. Soon the walls close in again and the shade returns. It can be cold along this part if you've been in chest-deep water.

About 10.3 miles from the Wire Pass-Buckskin intersection, you come to the famous boulder jam (see Photo 3). The routes down the jam can change due to flash floods. The safest route down is on the far left (facing down canyon) as indicted by the arrow in Photo 3. There's a 12-foot vertical chimney that had black webbing anchored to a boulder. Those experienced with down climbing chimneys will not need the webbing. The first person down can help the others. The other routes down the boulder jam had questionable ropes when I was there. Wet shoes and sand on the boulders make all of the other routes tricky. Again, this can change due to flash floods and the amount of water in the canyon.

Just beyond the boulder jam, a tiny seep starts out of the rock. This is easily missed, but if found, is an excellent source of water. A mile and a quarter beyond the boulder jam, you come to a great campsite on the left. This is a popular site for backpackers. Another 0.25 of a mile and you arrive at the confluence of Paria Canyon and Buckskin. Don't expect marching bands and neon lights. It's the only opening in the last 11 miles. Simply turn left into Paria Canyon. At first, it's much the same as Buckskin,

PHOTO 3

PHOTO 4

with towering walls and fairly narrow. At 0.75 of a mile up Paria Canyon, you come to Slide Arch, where a huge block of sandstone fell, creating an arch along the right side of the canyon wall (see Photo 4).

Beyond Slide Arch, the canyon widens, but there are still plenty of photo opportunities. Some Wave-like rock formations appear along this part of the canyon. Two miles from Whitehouse trailhead (end of the hike) you'll pass under power lines. Continue two miles and look for a path off to the right. It's marked by a cairn (Waypoint 2). As soon as you step onto the path you can see Whitehouse trailhead and hopefully your car.

WAYPOINTS:
1. 37.0197N / 112.0028W
2. 37.07917N / 111.89056W

The Wave
Route

Trailhead: Wire Pass, marked
Distance: 6 miles, up and back
Elevation gain: 350 feet
Elevation of peak: None
Time: 3 hours+ time you spend at the Wave
Difficulty: 2
Danger level: 2
Class: 2
How easy to follow: 3
Children: Yes, if experienced hikers
Waypoints (WGS 84): See page 184
Permits: $7 per person
Best season: Spring or autumn (extremely hot during summer)

Driving Directions

From Kanab, UT, head east on US89 for 37 miles and turn right onto the signed House Rock Valley Road. It's between mile markers 26 and 25. It's also labeled Road 700 on some maps. After a few hundred yards, it becomes a gravel road. Drive 8 miles to the signed Wire Pass trailhead parking area. There's a pit toilet at the parking area.

A high-clearance vehicle is recommended. The road becomes impassable after a heavy rain.

Note: Your mileage might vary slightly due to tire size and air pressure.

Permits: Permits are hard to acquire. Only 20 hikers per day are allowed in the Wave. Group size is limited to 6 people. Your best strategy is to obtain permits via the Internet. You can get permits up to four months in advance.

Example: On July 1, you can get permits for October. The permits become available at noon or 1 p.m. (MST) on the first day of each month. They seem to change the time to keep people guessing. When I got permits on July 1 for October 4, the entire month was booked by 12:55 p.m. Be at your computer at noon four months before you want to go. Here's the website: www.blm.gov/az/paria/checklist.cfm.

For the area choose: Coyote Buttes North.

Walk-in Permits: These are issued via a lottery system and are good only for the following day, not the same day. From November 15 to March 15, you can try for walk-in permits at the Kanab Ranger Station, corner of 100 East Street and 300 North in Kanab, UT. It's open Monday through Friday. You get permits for Saturday, Sunday, and Monday on Friday. From March 16 to November 14, walk-in permits are available at Paria Contact (Ranger) Station, between mile markers 20 and 21 on UT89. It's open seven days a week.

Permits are mailed to the group leader. While hiking, the group leader must have the permit attached to his or her daypack. Tear off the upper part of the permit and put it in the window of your car. It serves as a parking pass.

Comments: The Wave is a must-see phenomenon! The sandstone looks like a wave frozen in time. It's an easy walk to the Wave and adventurous hikers can explore canyons, cones, and washes for hours. Photographers from all over the world hike to the Wave for that once-in-a-lifetime photo. The route below is probably the shortest and most direct way to the Wave.

Lodging: There are lots of motels in Kanab. We stayed at Parry Lodge, the choice of many Hollywood cast and crew while filming in the area; 800/748-4104.

The Hike: From the parking area, cross the road to the Wire Pass trailhead sign. The trail starts just to the right of the sign. There's a register for Buckskin Gulch hikers. The trail soon drops into Coyote Wash. Walk east (left) in the wash about 0.5 of a mile to an old road along the right side of the wash (Waypoint 1). There's a sign indicating that this is the Coyote Buttes Special Management Area. Follow the road up a hill to the register for the Wave. Log your permit number in the register, then continue on the road less than 100 yards and take a right at the fork. Photo 1 shows the sandstone ridge you'll scramble up and over. When the trail descends

PHOTO 2

into a wash, go right about 10 yards and scramble up and over the north end of a ridge; see Photo 2 (Waypoint 2). Stay to the east (left) of the ridge as you head south toward the Wave. In a few hundred yards, pass to the right of the Twin Buttes in Photo 3. Shortly, you'll cross a down

TWIN BUTTES

PHOTO 3

barbed wire fence. Off in the distance you can see a dark crack (see Photo 4). The Wave sits just below the crack. Hike south toward the Wave. You'll walk up a sandy hill (Waypoint 3) a few hundred yards before the Wave (see Photo 5). Make sure to scramble up and into Stans' Cones by hiking around the far side of them to an easy entrance.

PHOTO 4

PHOTO 5

Continue less than 100 yards to the Wave (Waypoint 4). There's a lot to see and photograph in the area. Adventurous hikers can scramble up (class 2/3) to the window above the dark crack by scrambling up to the right of the crack, then cutting back to the left above the crack to the window.

To Return: Retrace your steps.

WAYPOINTS:
1. 37.01997 N / 112.01803 W
2. 37.01436 N / 112.01064 W
3. 36.99809 N / 112.00625 W
4. 36.99543 N / 112.00581 W

Introduction to Escalante, Utah

Grand Staircase-Escalante National Monument spans nearly 1.9 million acres of public lands in southern Utah. Hidden within are arches, plateaus, and canyons waiting to be explored. Coyote Gulch backpack is considered by many as the best backpack in the region.

I've included information about permits, what to bring, cautions, and fast facts in the actual hike, so I won't duplicate it here. I also included a cool optional hike to Stevens Arch, well worth doing. And if you buy this book in the next five minutes, I'll throw in how to climb out of the canyon at Jacob's Arch. Now you only have four minutes.

The land is managed by the BLM and is on Mountain Time. A self-issued permit is required, but it's free. There are no restricted hours for hiking or backpacking. This is a great backpack with incredible scenery and plenty of water sources. Have fun and write!

Lower Calf Creek Falls
Trail

Trailhead: Calf Creek Recreation Area, marked
Distance: 6.2 miles, up and back
Elevation gain: 250 feet
Elevation of peak: None
Time: 3 to 4 hours
Difficulty: 2
Danger level: 2
Class: 1
How easy to follow: 2
Children: Yes
Waypoints (WGS 84): See page 189
Fees: $2.00 self registration fee
Best season: Spring and autumn

Driving Directions

From the town of Escalante, UT, continue on UT12 another 14.4 miles and turn left at the signed Calf Creek Recreation Area. Park in the day use parking area (Waypoint 1).

Comments: This is one of the foremost day hikes in the Escalante region. Great views, an easy to follow trail, and a year-round, 126-foot, revitalizing waterfall make this a great hike. If attempting this hike during the summer months, start in mid-afternoon. A good part of your hike back to the trailhead will be in the shade. Restrooms and drinking water are available at the trailhead. Dogs are allowed on the trail if on a leash.

A brochure is keyed to 17 numbered posts along the trail, indicating vegetation and geologic features. We didn't find the brochure, but the posts serve as landmarks.

Lodging: Calf Creek Campground, $7 per night.
www.publiclands.org/explore/site.php?id=1338
Various motels in Escalante, UT.
www.go-utah.com/Escalante/Hotels/

The hike: Walk the paved road following signs through the campground 0.2 of a mile to the signed trailhead on the left side of the road. As you turn onto the trail, there's a self-register on your left. The wide and often sandy trail starts with an easy grade, allowing you to look at the expanse of sandstone formations. The terrain looks similar to Red Rock Canyon, outside of Las Vegas. The trail heads north along the west slopes above Calf Creek. Numerous spur paths lead down to Calf Creek.

PHOTO 1

At one mile or so, the trail becomes difficult to follow as it drops into a dry wash. Most hikers go to the left, instead of following the poorly defined trail to the right and up sandstone stairs.

The trail continues north past a boxed-in canyon. If you lose the trail, look for Post Number 7. The trail bends to the east (right), crosses a branch of the creek, and enters a different fork of the canyon. The 200-foot canyon walls provide shade in the late afternoon. Soon, you'll be hiking within several feet of the creek. If you look hard, you might just see some brook trout in the crystal clear water. As the trail draws closer to the waterfall, you can hear a rumbling in the distance. Trees provide plenty of shade during the last few hundred yards to the waterfall. As you turn a corner you get your first glimpse through the trees of the waterfall.

The trail ends in an amphitheater among the 126-foot roaring waterfall as seen in Photo 1, (Waypoint 2). You'll notice it's much cooler at the waterfall. Don't expect to have the waterfall all to yourself. This is a very popular hike.

To Descend: Retrace your steps.

WAYPOINTS:
1. 37.7939 N / 111.4150 W
2. 37.8292 N / 111.4200 W

Introduction to Coyote Gulch Backpack

Coyote Gulch is considered one of the best backpacks in the Escalante region. Great scenery, lots of water, and a relatively easy route make this trip a favorite. The backpack begins at Red Well trailhead. By departing from this trailhead, instead of Hurricane Wash trailhead, you reach the gulch and water sooner—a big plus if it's warm.

Coyote Gulch can be crowded during the peak seasons (spring and fall). If you can tolerate heat, summer is a great time to experience the gulch. You won't need a tent, warm clothes, or even a sleeping bag if you really want to go light. Also, you might have the place to yourself.

Warning: You're on your own while backpacking Coyote Gulch. If you or someone in your party gets hurt, help is hours away. This backpack isn't dangerous, but any backpack can be dangerous if common sense and adequate planning aren't incorporated.

Brief Overview

Day 1—Leave from Red Well trailhead and hike seven miles to Jacob Hamlin Arch.

Day 2—Hike four miles to the second campsite; optional side trip to Stevens Arch.

Day 3—Hike 11 miles back out to the trailhead.

Fast Facts

Mileage: 22 miles (26 miles to river)
Time: 3 days
Elevation gain: 900 feet on the way out
Water: Abundant
Best season: Spring and fall
Permits: Required for camping (no charge)
Trailhead: Red Well
Fees: None
Time Zone: Mountain Time
Dogs: Must be on a leash
Closest Town: Escalante—gas and groceries available
Contact Information: Escalante Ranger Station, Glen Canyon National Recreation Area, P.O. Box 511, Escalante, Utah, 84726; 435/826-4315 or 435/826-5499. Open 7 days a week—8 a.m. to 4:30 p.m. (closed on weekends during winter months). Located on the right side of the road in the town of Escalante, UT.
Emergencies: Call Escalante Interagency Office at 435/826-5499 or Glen Canyon National Recreation Area 24-hour dispatch at 800/582-4351.

Permits

Permits are self-issued at the trailhead. You can also get permits at the ranger station in Escalante and check on weather conditions. *Flash flooding is a serious problem*. The roads can be washed out. You can call the ranger station in Escalante at 435/826-4315. There is also a ranger station in Boulder, Utah. *Group size is limited to 12.*

Backpacking Store

If you forget anything, you're in luck. In the middle of the town of Escalante, there's a great store. From camp stoves to topo maps, **Escalante Outfitters** has what you need: 320 Main Street (you drive right by it on the way to the trailhead), 435/826-4266; Monday through Saturday 8 a.m.-10 p.m.; Sundays 8 a.m.-9 p.m.; www.escalanteoutfitters.com.

Weather

www.weather.com/outlook/recreation/outdoors/local/USUT0075?
from=recentsearch

Things to Watch Out For

Sand: It's everywhere and it will get in your water shoes. Sock liners help prevent your feet from getting cut by the sand. The top of my toes looked like someone used sandpaper on them. Wearing sock liners stopped the sand grinding against my toes by 80%.

Deer flies and gnats: These can be a problem in early summer. We had deer flies during our backpack in early July. They weren't bad enough to wear long pants and a long-sleeve shirt, though some hikers may want to.

Rattlesnakes: Watch where you place your hands while climbing. Snakes are most active from April to October, though you usually won't see them during the height of the summer; it's too hot.

Scorpions: These creatures crawl into things at night. Shake out shoes and clothing before you dress.

Poison ivy: This grows near the springs. It has three shiny leaves. Most people aren't allergic to it, but if you are, it can ruin a trip.

What to Bring

Blister kit: Just about everyone gets blisters. Moleskin, Spyroflex, duct tape, and a needle are the main components of blister prevention and cure.

ID and Money: You might want money for dinner in Escalante on the drive back. Escalante Outfitters has a restaurant with some of the best pizza I've ever eaten.

Food: If backpacking for three days, you'll need six to seven meals, plus snacks.

Day 1: Dinner (breakfast and lunch can be eaten at home or on the road).

Day 2: Breakfast, lunch, and dinner.

Day 3: Breakfast and lunch (dinner can be eaten on the drive home).

Mountain House freeze dried meals are considered the best. Most people repackage them to save space. Walmart Supercenters have good prices, though limited selection.

Stove and fuel: To cook the Mountain House meals.

Matches: Waterproof are always a good choice.

Mess kit: You can eat your meals out of the Mountain House packages. If so, all you'll need is a spoon or fork and one pot.

Water: Although there's water along much of the hike, you'll need to start with water. Remember, drink before you become thirsty. There are springs at the campsites—no need to treat. All other water must be treated or filtered.

Water filter: You'll need to filter water until you reach the spring near the campsite.

Sports drink: Buy Gatorade powder and repackage with baggies. When you come to water, fill an empty bottle with the powder and add water. This way you'll have Gatorade throughout the backpack. Three days of nothing but water gets old.

Daypack: There are several on the market. If you do any of the side trips, you will want a daypack.

Clothing: Depends on the month. Keep in mind you'll get wet. If summer, shorts and T-shirts will be all you need.

Camp towel: Dry off after bathing and swimming.

Sunglasses: Protect your eyes from the bright sun.

Sunscreen: Protect your skin from the sun. Apply often.

Hat: Keeps you cool and protects you from the sun.

Boots: You'll be walking less than five miles on dry land (in and out). The rest of the backpack is in water. A lightweight hiking shoe is sufficient. Even more important is a water shoe. Teva has several models.

Hiking Socks: Bring at least two pairs. After the first two miles, you'll be walking in water and might want to take them off.

Sock Liners: Mandatory if you wear water shoes. Sock liners protect your feet from the grinding sand.

Tevas (optional): Great for around the campsite.

Toiletries: Toothbrush, deodorant, etc.

Bear Canister: Although not mandatory, there are mice. Use a bear canister or hang your food.

Tent: Depends. If it's warm, you don't need it.

Sleeping bag or bivvy sack: Needed in spring and fall. You might go without in summer.

Thermarest: A nice luxury; however, both campsites are sandy.

Hiking Poles: Personal preference.

Mileage Charts

Day 1
Start of stream	2 miles
Jacob Hamlin Arch—Campsite	7 miles

Day 2
Pinnacle	0.7 mile
Coyote Natural Bridge	1.7 miles
First Waterfall and Cliff Arch	3.2 miles
Second Waterfall	3.8 miles
Alcove Campsite	4 miles

Day 3
Back to trailhead	11 miles

Coyote Gulch to Escalante River
Route

Trailhead: Red Well, marked
Distance: 26 miles, up and back
Elevation lost: 900 feet
Time: 3 days
Difficulty: 3
Danger level: 3 (dehydration and flash flooding)
Class: 1
How easy to follow: 2
Children: No
Waypoints: Not needed
Fees: None
Permits: Required for camping (self-issued—no cost)
Best season: Spring and autumn (summer if you like heat and dislike crowds)

Driving Directions

From the town of Escalante, Utah, drive on UT12 almost six miles and turn right on the Hole in the Rock Road. Drive 30 miles on this gravel road to the signed junction for Red Well trailhead. Turn left and drive 1.5 miles to the signed trailhead.

Comments: This is one of the best backpacking trips in Escalante. With water literally under your feet and abundant campsites, logistically it's an easy backpack. Soaring cliffs, waterfalls, and amazing arches make this a must-do adventure. There are two optional side trips (hikes) that are also must-dos. The first climbs out of the canyon at Jacob Hamlin Arch. You look down almost 300 feet on your campsite. The second side trip is to Stevens Arch. You'll be standing under the arch.

Water: Water is abundant; you're walking in the stream most of the trip. There are springs at both campsites. All other water needs to be filtered or treated. Bring enough water for the first two miles; they're dry and hot during summer months.

The Hike: The trail begins at the sign, "Hikers Obtain Permits Here" (see Photo 1). Follow the wide trail east several hundred yards. It then narrows to a single track trail and soon descends steeply into a wide wash. Continue east in the dry wash. Before long the wash becomes vegetated. A little beyond two miles, you reach a stream, which you follow the rest of the backpack. At this point, you can walk in the water (ankle deep normally) or follow paths on either side of the stream. Walking in the water is the preferred route (it's more scenic) and doesn't damage the surrounding vegetation. Change into your water shoes here. Even if you follow the paths, you cross the stream numerous times.

Continue east down the canyon. If in doubt, follow the water. It flows toward Escalante River. At about seven miles, you pass a sign pointing to a pit toilet. Jacob Hamlin Arch comes into view at this point (see Photo 2). There are two campsites here, both under alcoves. The first one is next to the arch, the other just around the bend. The far campsite is the best (see Photo 3). It's also under an alcove, closer to the spring, and has its own pit toilet. The spring is located about 300 yards downstream on the

PHOTO 2

left side (see Photo 4). Be careful of poison ivy at the spring. Most people aren't allergic to it, but it can be a problem for those who are. The pit toilet is across from the spring up on a hill. Don't be lazy; please use it! A sign points to the trail, which goes up a hill to the pit toilet. This is the end of Day 1.

PHOTO 3

PHOTO 4

Optional Side Trip: This hike climbs above the alcove. You can actually hang your head (carefully) over the alcove and look down almost 300 feet to the campsite.

From the campsite, walk downstream about 350 yards, passing the springs to the sign for the pit toilet. Just to the right of the sign, a sand-stone shoulder reaches the ground (see Photo 5). Scramble up the shoul-der (class 3, exposed). It's a friction climb. After the first 100 feet, the climbing becomes easier. Once the grade lessens, veer right as shown in Photo 6. Soon the lower part of Jacob Hamlin Arch comes into view and it's apparent you're on top of the alcove. Hike about 200 yards to a low point along the sandstone. Walk near the edge, lie down, and carefully extend your head out over the alcove. It's an amazing view (see Photo 7).

This side hike should only take 30 minutes round trip, excluding time for taking photos and enjoying the scenery.

PHOTO 5

As you look around, all you see are acres of sandstone. The terrain is easy and you could go explore for hours. Just make sure to find your way back to the down climb. You might see cairns if you head SE. The cairns mark a route from Forty Mile Ridge trailhead to Jacob Hamlin Arch.

PHOTO 6

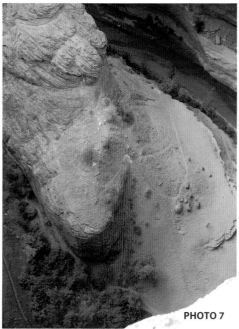

PHOTO 7

PHOTO 8

Day 2
Distance: 4 miles
Time: 3 to 5 hours

This is the best part of Coyote Gulch. You'll see waterfalls, arches, and a natural bridge. Since it's a short distance to your next campsite, take your time and make sure to see everything.

From Jacob Hamlin Arch, continue downstream, passing the springs and the sign for the pit toilet. Around every bend there's something to see. At 0.7 of a mile from Jacob Hamlin Arch, you pass a pinnacle. In another mile, you walk under Coyote Natural Bridge, a testament to the power of water and time.

A little farther down the canyon, boulders litter the stream. Although easy to get around, it's awkward with a heavy pack. Stay just to the left of the stream to get around the boulders. Just beyond the boulders, you come upon the first waterfall. Bypass it by following a trail to the left of the stream. Cliff Arch, also known as Jug Handle Arch, is visible from the first waterfall (see Photo 8). It's halfway up the north wall.

Continue downstream about 0.5 of a mile, passing a sandstone tower rising sharply from the canyon floor. A short distance beyond the tower, you come to the top of a 15-foot waterfall, the most forceful in the canyon (see Photo 9). If you want to cool off in the waterfall, descend via a steep and loose path to the right of the waterfall.

PHOTO 9

From the second waterfall, hike downstream 100 yards to the third waterfall. Bypass this waterfall on the right side via a ledge. About halfway along the ledge, descend into the stream. You might want to take off packs and pass them down. Continue downstream a 100 yards, passing a spring part way up on the north wall. Forget about filling a water bottle here. There's a better spring just beyond the campsite, 200 yards away. An alcove, smaller than the alcove at the first campsite, appears on the right side of the canyon (see Photo 10). *This is your campsite.* A pool created by a small waterfall lies less than 100 yards downstream from the campsite. Across from the waterfall is a sign for another pit toilet, which sits at the top of a hill.

There's a reliable but hard-to-find spring just beyond the pool. The spring is located below what appears to be the beginning of a large arch on the north wall. From the pool continue in the stream about 200 yards to a small opening to the left. It's easily missed. Follow a faint path to a sandstone wash. Hike up the wash 40 yards to the spring, which is visible once in the wash.

PHOTO 10

Escalante River and Stevens Arch

Side Trip: Optional
Distance: 4 miles, up and back
Time: 2 to 3 hours, up and back
Difficulty: 2
Danger level: 3 (dehydration)
Class: 3
How easy to follow: 1

Comments: Stevens Arch is magnificent. If you do this hike in the morning during the summer months, you'll be in the shade. *Do not attempt this hike if the river is flooded.*

The Hike: From the campsite head downstream passing the waterfall and spring. The canyon narrows and sandstone walls increase in height as you head toward Escalante River. About 0.4 of a mile before the river, the canyon becomes blocked by boulders and logs. Follow a path that heads south (right), making sure to stay on the lowest path. The sandy path gives way to sandstone ledges that you must traverse (see Photo 11). They're exposed, but it's really just class 1. Once across the ledges, an easy down climb leads back to the stream. A stump has been placed at the down climb to assist hikers. Continue another 0.25 of a mile to the river.

PHOTO 11

PHOTO 12

At the river, walk north (left) about 250 yards. As you walk in the river, Stevens Arch appears (see Photo 12). On the right bank of the river, look for a small opening through the trees by boulders. This avoids brush. Once beyond the trees, head south (right) following a faint footpath toward a boulder avalanche. The path travels to the far side of the boulders and ascends the steep slope. It becomes easier to follow and cairns mark the route. The path climbs to a bench just shy of huge vertical walls. Head north on an easy to follow path to the arch. Just before the arch is an easy class 3 move that leads to and through the arch. There's a spectacular 360-degree view from the arch. The deep canyon on the far side of the arch is Stevens Canyon.

Retrace your steps back to the campsite.

Day 3
Distance: 11 miles
Time: 6 hours to all day

Basically, you're retracing your steps back out. Fill your bladder from the spring before leaving or have a way of treating water. When you get close to Jacob Hamlin Arch, you can fill up again at the springs. Walking on paths is faster, but you'll still walk in and cross the stream several times. The only confusing area is near Hurricane Wash, which is signed, though you might miss it. When you see the sign, veer right. It might seem like you're walking in a circle, but you are on the correct route. As you hike through a narrow passage, just beyond the Hurricane Wash sign, veer left when the canyon divides again. When in doubt, follow the water. You will be walking against the current.

Eventually, the stream dries up (make sure you have plenty of water) and you end up in a wide dry wash. Look for the obvious trail leading up a steep hill in about a half-mile after entering the dry wash. Follow the trail back to the trailhead.

Introduction to Zion National Park

Zion Canyon, Utah's first national park (established in 1909), is home to peaks and pinnacles, canyons and washes, and unbelievable scenery. From easy trails to canyoneering to remote peaks, Zion is a must-visit area. Don't forget to bring your camera.

The five hikes in this chapter are the best Zion has to offer. Angels Landing is one of the most popular hikes in the country! The last quarter-mile travels an exposed ridge with lots of air on both sides. Bridge Mountain is one of the toughest peaks in Zion. Remote and airy, it'll challenge any peak bagger. Observation Point offers some of the best views in Zion. The Narrows is world-famous. Walls tower more than 2,000 feet as you walk in the Virgin River. If you're into canyoneering the Subway is the perfect beginner's canyoneering adventure.

Zion Canyon is managed by the National Park Service. Permits aren't required for most hikes; however the Subway and the Narrows do require permits. There's a $25 per vehicle entrance fee, good for seven days. All National Park passes are accepted. There are no restricted hours for hiking the trails. The Visitor Center, located at just inside the park's south entrance, is open 8 a.m.-8 p.m. daily in the summer; 8 a.m.-6 p.m. spring and autumn, and 8 a.m. to 4:30 p.m. during winter months. Zion Canyon is on Mountain Time.

Tip: If you have nine or more people in your group, you can stay in the group site at Watchman Campground for just $3 per person.

PHOTO 1

Angels Landing, West Rim
Trail

Trailhead: Grotto Picnic Area on the Scenic Drive Road, marked
Distance: 5 miles, up and back
Elevation gain: 1,488 feet
Elevation peak: 5,790 feet
Time: 3-4 hours, up and back
Difficulty: 3
Danger level: 4
Class: 3
How easy to follow: 1
Children: No
Waypoints: Not needed
Fees: $25 entrance fee per car. Good for seven days. All national park passes accepted.
Best season: Spring and autumn

Driving Directions

From Springdale, UT, you have two options: Park in Springdale and catch the free shuttle (look for "Shuttle Parking" signs in Springdale) to the entrance to Zion National Park (parking is very limited at the Visitor Center) and walk five minutes to the Visitor Center (fee for walk-ins is $12 per person good for seven days) or drive one mile from Springdale to the entrance to Zion

National Park. Take the first right and follow signs to the Visitor Center parking. Another free shuttle bus leaves from the Visitor Center every 7 to 10 minutes and drives to the trailheads.

Fee schedule:

www.nps.gov/zion/planyourvisit/feesandreservations.htm

Refer to the map on this page: www.nps.gov/zion/planyourvisit/upload/Springdale%20Shuttle%20Parking%20Map.pdf.

Note: Zion Canyon Scenic Drive, where most of the trailheads are located, is closed to cars from April to November. During the off season (winter), you can drive your car to the trailheads.

Comments: Angel's Landing is one of the most popular hikes in Zion. The summit feels like you're standing on top of the world. It's not for anyone scared of heights. Chains have been installed along the exposed part of the ridge to help hikers feel more comfortable during the ascent.

The Hike: The trail immediately crosses to the north (far) side of the Virgin River via a bridge, then divides. Go north (right) at the divide and follow the paved trail as it uses switchbacks to climb. Although the south wall of Refrigerator Canyon looks sheer, the trail snakes along the south wall.

The trail crosses a wooden bridge and heads north into Refrigerator Canyon. The canyon offers shade and cooler temperatures on hot days. Short steep switchbacks climb south toward Angels Landing. Here's where you can appreciate the incredible amount of work it took to build this trail. Soon the trail levels and divides; continue south on the dirt trail. The West Rim Trail heads north to Scout Lookout before going into the backcountry.

From here the hike turns into scramble along an exposed ridge. It's still 0.5 of a mile to the top. Chains have been placed along part of the route and footholds have been cut into the sandstone. The exposure is mild compared to some of the hikes in Red Rock, but for first-timers it may be challenging (see Photo 1).

The last 100 yards are steep and exhilarating. At the top of Angels Landing, you have a wonderful 360-degree view of Zion Canyon. To the west stands Cathedral Mountain; to the north lies the Narrows and Observation Point. Cable Mountain is out to the west. The Scenic Drive lies almost 1,400 feet below to the south.

To descend: Retrace your steps.

PHOTO 1

Bridge Mountain
Route

Trailhead: Canyon Overlook parking lot, unmarked and closed to cars
Distance: 7.5 miles, up and back
Elevation gain: 3,000 feet
Elevation of peak: 6,803 feet
Time: 8-9 hours, up and back
Difficulty: 5
Danger level: 5
Class: 4
How easy to follow: 4
Children: No
Waypoints (WGS 84): See page 216
Fees: $25 per vehicle good for 7 days; Golden Eagle pass accepted.
Best season: Spring and autumn

Driving Directions   From Springdale, UT, drive one mile to the entrance of Zion National Park. Continue on Route 9 (do *not* turn onto the Scenic Road) and drive through the famous Mt. Carmel Tunnel. Drive beyond the Canyon Overlook parking lot, which is now closed to cars, about a quarter-mile and park at an unnamed parking lot on the left side of the road. Parking here is limited.

Comments: Bridge Mountain is one of the premier peaks in Zion. Due to the exposure along the route, it has seldom been climbed. From the summit you have a great view of Zion Canyon. Once in Hepworth Wash, this route differs from the Bridge Mountain Arch route. Only hikers with experience traversing very exposed ledges should attempt this route.

Tip: Due to bright sun and whitish rock found on Bridge Mountain, make sure to wear sunglasses to protect your eyes.

Lodging: Watchman Campground, $16 per night. I have camped here several times.

www.nps.gov/zion/planyourvisit/campgrounds.htm

Various motels in Springdale, UT (one mile from Zion).

www.tripadvisor.com/Hotels-g61001-Springdale_Utah-Hotels.html

The Hike: Walk back down the road to the parking lot just before the Mt. Carmel Tunnel on the left. The unmark trail begins just to the right of the bathroom. Descend into Pine/Clear Creek, walk 25 yards SE (left), and scramble up the slickrock to get around the dry waterfall as seen in Photo 1. Follow a hiker's path down into Gifford Canyon.

PHOTO 2

Hike about 0.75 of a mile and exit the canyon to the west (right; see Photo 2, Waypoint 1). Scramble up steep slickrock heading south (left) of the dome in Photo 3. Follow cairns to a wall that stands below the dome. (At this point you can't see the dome.) Head south (left) on a path that parallels the wall. Instead of continuing on the path that soon becomes very loose, look for a path to the left. Follow this path up a vegetated shoulder about 75 yards where the terrain levels out. The path continues and heads SW to another wall. Head north (right) to gain the wall. The path fades here, but there are occasional cairns. Once up, the terrain soon changes to sandstone. Walk west sev-

PHOTO 3

eral hundred yards, following cairns, and gain a sandy plateau. An unnamed peak comes into view (see Photo 4).

The next part of the route drops into an east-west-heading canyon;

UNNAMED PEAK

PHOTO 4

however, there's a class 5 dry fall near the start of the canyon. To bypass it, descend north from the plateau, crossing a bowl. Continue north and parallel an ill-defined ridge until it becomes a class 3 scramble (see Photo 5). Climb over the ridge (Waypoint 2) and descend steep slickrock into an east/west canyon. Hike about 0.33 of a mile down the scenic east-west canyon until it bends sharply to the south (left). Just before that point, a path starts to the right and cuts northwest to Hepworth Wash. Hike north about 300 yards in Hepworth Wash, where you cross to the west (left) side of the wash.

PHOTO 5

BRIDGE MOUNTAIN

PHOTO 6

Leave the wash and head NW directly for Bridge Mountain (see Photo 6). There are occasional paths to follow. Drop into a small east-west wash and hike west a short distance to Waypoint 3. From here you can see two ramps ascending toward the sky; take the right-most ramp (see Photo 7). Scramble up the ramp until it becomes too steep and drop into the chute

PHOTO 7

to the left. Climb sandy ledges in the chute trying not to get too cut up from brush until you can exit to the right. Continue up the same direction on easy ground to a steep wall that blocks further progress. Traverse

PHOTO 8

left on an exposed ledge to the tree in Photo 8. Just beyond the tree, climb four feet onto another ledge system and once again traverse exposed ledges to a small cairn. Angle back to the right on a series of ledges where you'll find the rock less steep. From here scramble north up easy rock to the summit block. Climb the class 2/3 rock as shown in Photo 9. Once up hike west over easy rock less than 200 yards to the summit (Waypoint 4).

To Descend: Retrace your steps and look for

cairns. If you are only a few feet off, you could find yourself down climbing class 5 rock!

PHOTO 9

WAYPOINTS:
1. 37.20302 N / 112.93802 W
2. 37.20011 N / 112.94744 W
3. 37.20333 N / 112.96427 W
4. 37.20599 N / 112.96637 W

OBSERVATION POINT

Observation Point, East Rim
Trail

Trailhead: Weeping Rock parking lot, marked
Distance: 8 miles, up and back
Elevation gain: 2,148 feet
Elevation of peak: 6,508 feet
Time: 4-5 hours, up and back
Difficulty: 3
Danger level: 1
Class: 1
How easy to follow: 1
Children: No
Waypoints: Not needed
Fee: $25 per vehicle good for 7 days; Golden Eagle pass accepted.
Best season: Spring and autumn

Driving Directions

From Springdale, UT, you have two options: Park in Springdale and catch the free shuttle (look for "Shuttle Parking" signs in Springdale) to the entrance to Zion National Park (parking is very limited at the Visitor Center) and walk five minutes to the Visitor Center (fee for walk-ins is $12 per person good for seven days) or drive one mile from Springdale to the entrance to Zion National Park. Take the first right and follow signs to the Visitor Center parking. Another free shuttle bus drives leaves from the Visitor Center every 7 to 10 minutes and drives to the trailheads. Take the shuttle bus to the Weeping Rock parking lot, the trailhead for this hike.

Fee schedule:

www.nps.gov/zion/planyourvisit/feesandreservations.htm

Refer to the map on this page: www.nps.gov/zion/planyourvisit/upload/Springdale%20Shuttle%20Parking%20Map.pdf.

Note: Zion Canyon Scenic Drive, where most of the trailheads are located, is closed to cars from April to November. During the off season (winter), you can drive your car to the trailheads.

Comments: From Observation Point, you get a different perspective of Zion Canyon. This classic hike should be on the list of anyone who wants to learn about the mountains and peaks in Zion Canyon.

The Hike: The signed and paved East Rim Trail uses switchbacks to climb toward a giant amphitheatre, which makes up the SE face of Cable Mountain. The grade along this part of the trail is moderate. Observation Point is visible from the trail at this point. In a half-mile the trail forks; continue straight on the East Rim Trail. The trail continues climbing east toward the amphitheater. In one mile, the trail weaves through the towering walls of Echo Canyon. Be sure to look down into the bottom of Echo Canyon. At places it's less than three feet wide. As the trail swings around the head of the canyon, you can drop down into the bottom of the canyon. This short side trip stops at a 50-foot drop.

The trail enters a wash and the canyon tapers into a magnificent slot canyon. As you exit the slot canyon, you have a great view of the mountain the trail eventually traverses.

A bridge provides a way across the deep slot canyon. The landscape changes dramatically as the trail climbs NE. The slickrock disappears; the terrain is now filled with scrub and manzanita. At two miles you come upon two trail signs, one stating Observation Point is two miles away and the other marking the trail to Cable Mountain. I didn't see a trail to Cable Mountain, but it must be there.

The East Rim Trail heads west, using numerous switchbacks to climb the steep slickrock. At 6,400 feet, the trail stops climbing and travels NW across the face of the sandstone mountain. The view of Zion Canyon from the traverse is fantastic. The landscape changes from slickrock to typical high-desert terrain. Looking west (left), you can see your final destination: Observation Point. About a half-mile from where the trail started traversing, you intersect an unnamed trail that leads to the park boundary. Continue south a third of a mile to Observation Point.

The views from Observation point are some of the best in Zion. Be sure to walk over to the west side and look down at the Narrows. There are many spots to sit and admire the view.

To Descend: Retrace your steps.

PHOTO 1

The Narrows From Top to Bottom
Route

Trailhead: Chamberlain Ranch, marked
Distance: 16 or 17 miles, one way (depending where you start)
Elevation gain: -1679 feet (loss in elevation)
Time: A long day
Difficulty: 3
Danger level: 5 (flash floods)
Class: 1
How easy to follow: 1
Children: No
Waypoints: Not needed
Fees: $25 entrance fee per car. Good for seven days.
    Golden Eagle pass accepted.
Permits: Yes, see below.
Best season: Summer

Driving Directions

From Springdale, Ut, head north on UT9 about one mile to the south entrance of Zion park. At 12.2 miles, you exit the east entrance of the park. At 14.5 miles, turn left at on the signed North Fork Road. The road turns into a well-graded gravel road in about 4.5 miles. When you come to a closed gate, open it, drive through, and make sure to close it. Continue on the gravel road, following signs to the trailhead. Photo 1 is the trailhead. A normal car can drive to the trailhead, unless the road is wet. The road is closed when it snows.

Comments: The Narrows has been voted one of the top 10 hikes in the country. The Virgin River carved the 16-mile Narrows over a period of millions of years. Walls tower 2,000 feet above as you walk through the Narrows. You'll be walking in water at least 60% of the time. Maximum number of hikers in a group is 12.

Logistics: Since this is a one-way hike, you have to make plans on how to get to the trailhead. There are three practical methods.

The first and best way is to have someone drop you off at the trailhead. A high-clearance vehicle isn't necessary; the gravel road is in good shape. By doing this you avoid the shuttle, which costs money and adds an additional mile to the hike. Also, you don't have to get back to the trailhead after the hike to get your car, a real pain.

Taking the shuttle is the second option. Various companies shuttle hikers to the trailhead. The shuttle lets you off at the gate, not the trailhead. This adds an additional mile of walking to the hike.

Shuttle Company: *Zion Adventure Company*, $30 per person, 435/772-1001. Call one day in advance and ask for the Zion Narrows Shuttle.

Driving yourself is the third option. This does *not* require a special permit. (You still need a permit to hike the Narrows if starting at Chamberlain Ranch, the trailhead.) The downside of this option is you have to get your car at the end of the hike. It's about a 70-minute drive from Springdale to the trailhead. It takes well over two hours to get your car at the end of the hike and drive back down to Springdale.

Equipment: Rent equipment from Zion Adventure Outfitters. 435/772-1001, www.zionadventures.com/narrows2.htm.

For $16 you receive the proper boots (5.10 canyoneering boots), Neoprene socks, a wooden walking stick, and a map of the canyon. The above package is for warm weather. They also have a cold water wetsuit package. Visit the above website for more information. This company has been in business since 1996; they know what they're doing. Without the proper gear, you'll slip, probably fall, and bang your toes on some not-so-friendly rocks.

Note: You need to return the equipment by 8 p.m. the day of the hike.

Tip: Alternate your walking-stick hand to prevent blisters.

Bring a water filter. There's plenty of water, but it needs to be treated.
Polypro long-sleeve shirt. When we arrived at the trailhead at 7 a.m. in late June, it was 45 degrees. Remember, the trailhead is at 6,150 feet. It will warm up later in the day.

Permit: Required for hiking the Narrows from the top (Chamberlain Ranch) to the bottom (Temple of Sinawava). Permits are $5 *per group*, but limited to a maximum of 12 hikers per permit. Only 80 hikers are allowed to hike the Narrows top to bottom per day. You can reserve your permit online: zionpermits.nps.gov/backcountry.cfm?TripTypeID=3.

The above link takes you to the page where you can reserve your permit. In the drop-down box, select Virgin Narrows Dayuse Trail.

You can try for a walk-in permit the *day before* your hike at the Visitor Center. Permits are handled out on a first-come first-serve basis beginning at 5 pm. Good luck.

Cautions: People have died due to flash floods while hiking the Narrows. Fortunately, the Visitor Center will *not* issue permits if there is a good chance of rain, but the weather forecast is not always accurate.

Depending on the water level, hiking the Narrows can be relatively easy or a very arduous task. Luckily, a website measures the water flow through the Narrows and gives a rating of difficulty. The address is:

waterdata.usgs.gov/ut/nwis/uv/?site_no=09405500&PARAmeter_cd= 00065,00060,00010,72020

Note: The Narrows is called the North Fork of the Virgin River near Springdale.

Flow rate: 50 cfs or below	Easy
Flow rate: 50 to 100 cfs	Mild
Flow rate: 100 to 150 cfs	Moderate
Flow rate: 150 to 200cfs	Athletic
Flow rate: 200 to 300 cfs	Very difficult
Flow rate: 300 to 400 cfs	Near impossible
CFS = Cubic Feet per Second	

The Hike: From the trailhead, follow the road across a small creek. Cows are in the pasture next to the road. Hungry? At three miles from the trailhead, you'll pass the dilapidated Bulloch's Cabin. The road narrows to a footpath as it parallels the stream. Footpaths run along both sides of the stream (see Photo 2). It's easier to stay on the same side of the stream than to cross the stream at this point.

PHOTO 2

As you continue, the walls start forming a canyon (see Photo 3). Along this part of the hike you'll cross the stream numerous times; however, the water level is normally very low. If you haven't put on your canyoneering boots or Neoprene socks, this is the time to do it. From this point you can follow the path or walk in the water. You'll enter the Upper Narrows a little before six miles from the trailhead (see Photo 4).

PHOTO 3

PHOTO 4

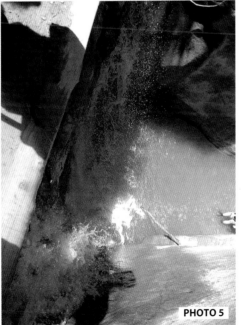

PHOTO 5

The canyon quickly widens and continues to 12-Foot Falls, which is about 8.5 miles from the trailhead (see Photo 5). Follow the path to the left of 12-Foot Falls. The canyon narrows and the walls increase in height. This is one of the more scenic parts of the Narrows. Continue to the convergence with Deep Creek (9 miles from the trailhead). The water level increases from this point. The Narrows gets two-thirds of its water from Deep Creek. As you proceed down river, you'll pass 12 signed campsites. At mile 11, you pass Big Springs (see Photo 6).

Just beyond Big Springs, the most dramatic part of the Narrows starts. Here the water becomes deep as you make your way downstream. A little over 13 miles from the trailhead, Orderville Canyon, a technical slot canyon, comes in from the east. In another mile you pass Mystery Canyon Falls, another slot canyon. You might see canyoneers rappelling 120 feet into the Narrows. You'll soon depart the river and follow the paved Riverside Walk one mile to the Temple of Sinawava, where you catch the shuttle. Bathrooms are near the shuttle stop.

PHOTO 6

PHOTO 1

The Subway via Russell Gulch
Route

Trailhead: Wildcat, marked
Distance: 9.5 miles, start to end
Elevation gain: About 500 feet
Time: 7+ hours, start to end
Difficulty: 3
Danger level: 5 (flash floods, very cold water)
Class: 4
Canyon Rating: 3B III
How easy to follow: 5
Children: No
Waypoints (WGS 84): See page 233
Fees: $25 entrance fee per car. Good for seven days. All national park passes accepted.
Permits: Yes, see below.
Best season: Late spring, early autumn
Equipment: 60 foot of rope or webbing, harness and a rappelling device, dry bag, wetsuit, towel, and water shoes. You can leave the harness and rappelling device at home if you are *very comfortable* handlining down vertical walls.

Driving Directions

From Springdale, UT, head south on Route 9 about 14 miles and turn right onto the signed Kolob Terrace Road. Drive 8.1 miles and leave a car at the signed *Left Fork* trailhead for the Subway. There's a restroom and trash container at this trailhead. You will end the hike here. Pile all the gear and hikers into the second car and continue up Kolob Terrace Road another 7.6 miles and turn right at the signed *Wildcat Trailhead*. There's a restroom and trash container at this trailhead also. Passenger cars can drive to both trailheads.

Comments: The Subway is one of the top 10 hikes in the country. It has it all: scenery, rock scrambling, swimming, and rappelling. It's a must-do hike! All mileages in the write-up below are estimates. In this type of terrain, it's impossible to know how far you've hiked with any accuracy.

Logistics: The best way to do this hike is to camp at Zion or get a motel room. Pick up your permit the day before at the Visitor Center in Zion. Since this is a *one-way hike*, you have to make plans on how to get to the trailheads. There are two practical methods.

The first and best way is to do your own car shuttle. See above.

Taking a shuttle bus is the second option. Various companies shuttle hikers to the trailheads. If you choose this option, you'll be hiking with lots of other people and can expect bottlenecks. The first option is much better.

Shuttle Company: *Zion Adventure Company*, $20 per person. Call for details: 435/772-1001.

Note: If you drive to the trailhead, get there at 9 a.m. Here's why: You want it to be warmer when you get to the cold swims and you want to avoid hikers from the shuttle buses. One of the shuttle buses drops off hikers at the trailhead around 7:30 a.m., the other around 9:30 a.m.

Equipment: Plain and simple: Rent equipment from Zion Adventure Outfitters. www.zionadventures.com/. For about $35, you receive Neoprene socks and a wetsuit. Try on the wetsuit before leaving the store. If it's too big, it's no good. This company has been in business since 1996; they know what they're doing.

Note: You need to return the equipment by 8 p.m. the day of the hike. Without the proper gear, you'll be very cold.

Permit: Required for day hiking the Subway. Permits cost $10 to $20 per person depending on group size, but are limited to a maximum of 12 hikers per permit. Only 50 hikers are allowed to hike the Subway each day. Permits are available by lottery and walk-in at the Visitor Center, located just beyond the south entrance (main) to the park. You can't miss it. Call 435/772-0170 for details. Since these requirements change, check the website: www.nps.gov/archive/zion/Backcountry/ReservationsAnd Permits.htm#calendar

Cautions: People have died due to flash floods while hiking the Subway. Check with rangers at the Visitor Center before hiking. We were asked for permits twice while on the hike. Keep your permit in your dry bag.

How to keep your items dry: Buy a dry bag. Put everything in it you don't want to get wet: car keys, wallet, food, extra clothes, camera, GPS, and towel. They cost around $20 and are very lightweight. You need to fold them three times to make sure water does not get in. When you see a dry bag, you'll understand.

How to float your daypack in the water: This is simple. Just use a dry bag. The air in the dry bag acts like a floatation device. Place the dry bag inside your daypack. That's all there is to it.

Lodging: Watchman Campground $16 per night. I've camped here several times.

www.nps.gov/zion/planyourvisit/campgrounds.htm

Various motels in Springdale, UT (one mile from Zion).

www.tripadvisor.com/Hotels-g61001-Springdale_Utah-Hotels.html

The Hike: From the signed trailhead, walk east, passing a signed turnoff for Hop Valley Trail and continue about a mile from the trailhead to the signed Northgate Peak Trail. Head right (south) 50 yards to the signed Subway route. Veer left onto the path. In 50 yards, the path gives way to slickrock, which is cairned after the first 40 yards. Russell Gulch is now visible (see Photo 1). A prominent trail begins at the end of the slickrock. Almost immediately the trail divides; take the right fork. The trail occasionally gives way to slickrock for short distances. Continue SE, following cairns to Photo 2. It gets a little tricky here to follow.

Continue to the cairn (Waypoint 1) in Photo 3, which marks the descent across Russell Gulch. You won't drop into the gulch for a while. Continue on cairned slickrock, going around a drop-off with water below. The path resumes, making a hard right, and soon gives way to more slickrock. Head for the saddle in Photo 4. Once near the saddle, hike just to the left of it to a well-placed cairn. Continue down the slickrock bowl on the other side of the saddle. At the end of the bowl, a path begins in the vegetation and heads SE.

The route curves to the right and descends steeply. Follow the path

GREATHEART MESA

PHOTO 2

as it ascends and Greatheart Mesa comes back into view. Shortly a huge log blocks the path. Take the spur path to the right where it rejoins the main trail in about 30 yards. Follow the path about 100 yards and turn right. This marks the *easily missed* descent into Russell Gulch. It's steep and loose (class 3) in places; see Photo 5 (Waypoint 2).

PHOTO 3

PHOTO 4

Navigation is now a piece of cake. You're now in Russell Gulch. Continue less than 100 yards to the intersection (confluence) of the Left Fork of the Subway. Turn *right* and the fun begins. Take your time and take lots of photos of the dramatic scenery.

PHOTO 5

Continue about 300 yards to the first of four obstacles: a huge boulder. Go to the far right side where an anchor has been placed. Use your rope or sling now. The trick is to go down *the easily missed hole.* It looks scary, but it's only 10 feet down. It's hard to see because it's dark (see Photo 6). The first person down can help the others. Continue to the first swim, which can be 20 yards long. Place everything in your dry bag and get ready to swim!

Keep your wetsuit on.

PHOTO 6

PHOTO 7

There are more cold-water swims and wading in waist-deep water. You'll come to the second obstacle: a chockstone jam in a narrow part of the canyon. Use your rope or webbing if none is present. There was a good anchor along the right wall. This is the easiest of the obstacles.

In about an hour, you come to Keyhole Falls, the third obstacle. This one is tricky, since there's water running down and no footholds. Again, there's an anchor along the right wall. Make sure to have a good grip on the webbing or rope (see Photo 7).

Soon, you enter the Subway section of the hike. It's really beyond belief. If you haven't already gotten your camera from your dry bag, do it now. You'll want to take photos from here on. You have one more section of deep water to cross (see Photo 8). I had my camera attached to my chest strap and it didn't get wet, but I'm over 6 feet tall. Once past that water, that's it for deep water. Get out of your wet suit. You'll be warmer.

You soon come to a

PHOTO 8

log jammed in a narrow crack with a big dropoff to your right. Use the log to get past and continue on the ledge 20 yards to the final obstacle. There are two bolts for the rappel. sixty feet of rope are needed here. You can handline it, but it'll be slick due to your wet shoes and sand. Once down, more photo opportunities are waiting, including several cascades. Be careful as some spots are very slippery.

Continue following the water by using paths or walking in the water. Around seven miles from the trailhead, there are two slabs of white rock with dinosaur tracks imbedded in them (Waypoint 3). They are to the right of the trail.

The water is gone now and the path becomes long. There's a small sign (Waypoint 4) to mark where you start the steep (300-foot) ascent to the trailhead. Once up the ascent, it's an easy walk on the trail as it weaves through a forest for less than a mile to the Left Fork trailhead, where you left a car.

WAYPOINTS:
1. 37.33136N / 113.04638W
2. 37.31828N / 113.04003W
3. 37.29953N / 113.06998W
4. 37.28885N / 113.08569W

NEW MEXICO

Introduction to New Mexico

Wheeler Peak is the highest in New Mexico (13,161 feet). It's part of the Sangre de Cristo range of the Rocky Mountains. The trailhead is located at Taos Ski Valley Lodge about 15 miles west of the town of Taos, New Mexico. Besides hiking, you can raft, mountain bike, horseback ride, rock climb, golf, and, of course, ski!

This is my favorite hike in New Mexico. Okay, I've only done one hike in New Mexico. But it's idyllic, traveling across high alpine meadows. Yes, it's trail the whole way, but you're up high with great vistas and plenty of nearby peaks that could perk your interest.

You might want to stay at one of the many lodges near the ski lodge. During the off season (summer), you can get a good deal. This way you can take a few days to explore and bag other nearby peaks. To put it another way, it's a long drive from anywhere, so it would be worthwhile to stay a few days and bag as many peaks as you can.

No permits are required and hours aren't restricted. Wheeler Peak and the surrounding area are managed by the U.S. Forest Service. New Mexico is on Mountain Time.

PHOTO 1

Wheeler Peak, Bull of the Woods
Trail

Trailhead: Taos Ski Valley Resort, marked
Distance: 16 miles, up and back
Elevation gain: 4,400 feet
Elevation peak: 13,161 feet
Time: 7-8 hours, up and back
Difficulty: 5
Danger level: 4 (thunderstorms)
Class: 1
How easy to follow: 1
Children: No
Waypoints (WGS 84): See page 242
Fees: None
Best season: Summer and early autumn

Driving Directions From the town of Taos, NM, head north on Pueblo Road/ NM522. When the road divides, veer left on to NM64 and continue four miles to the *first* traffic light. Turn right onto NM150/Ski Valley Rd. and drive 15 miles to Taos Ski Valley. At the big welcome sign, veer left to the upper parking lot. The trail begins by the sign in Photo 1.

Comments: Since Wheeler is the highest peak in New Mexico, it's a must-do for serious peak baggers. It stands in the southern end of the Sangre de Cristo range of the Rocky Mountains and it's named after U.S. Army Major George M. Wheeler, who surveyed much of New Mexico in the late 1870s. There are several routes to the summit. This is the standard route and the most scenic. The hike can be extremely windy. If hiking during the monsoon season (summer), get an early start and be off the peak before noon. Bring warm clothes and rain gear!

Note: New Mexico is on Mountain Time.

Lodging: Campsites from $17 per night.

lodging.uptake.com/camping/new_mexico/taos_ski_valley/340702175.html

Various condos and hotels, which have great deals during the off season (summer). www.skitaos.org/lodging/village_listings.php

The Hike: From the trailhead kiosk in Photo 1, follow the trail, crossing a gravel road to the official trailhead sign (Waypoint 1). There's a bathroom to the left, but it was closed when I was there. The trail divides in 50 yards; take the left fork. As the trail parallels a creek, look for ice hanging off branches above the creek during cooler months. It makes

PHOTO 2

for great photos. Stay on the main trail, avoiding all spur trails marked with a symbol of a horse.

This first part of the trail is shady and can be very cold in the morning. It also crosses private land, so make sure to stay on the trail. In a little less than a mile, you cross the creek via logs. When the trail widens, you'll be on Forest Road 79 (not marked) and hiking up Long Canyon. It's open here and the sun shines down on the road.

In two miles you come to a small pond at Bull of the Woods Pasture (10,860 feet). Veer right onto

Wheeler Peak Trail 90 as indicated by the sign. Continue on the road to the top of the hill to Red River Canyon Overlook. The road continues heading north and you get your first view of the Taos Ski Lodge almost 2,000 feet below. Continue to the top of the road where the route forks at about the three-mile point. Veer right, leaving the road onto the signed Wheeler Peak trail (see Photo 2).

The trail soon narrows to a single-track trail, heads south, and enters a forest. The forest is short-lived and the trail comes to a scenic meadow. It heads south across the west face of the Bull of the Woods Mountain. If it's windy, you'll feel it here. At 12,000 feet, you walk past a Wheeler Peak wilderness sign. Just beyond the sign, the rest of the route and Wheeler Peak come into view (see Photo 3).

WHEELER PEAK

PHOTO 3

Unfortunately, the trail loses about 500 feet as it drops into La Cal Basin. Look for bighorn sheep in this area. The trail crosses a small stream before entering another forest. This is the last water source and it's still three miles to the summit. The trail emerges from the forest and climbs the ridge via long switchbacks. At 12,800 feet, the trail comes to a saddle. Off to the east lies Horseshoe Lake.

The trail climbs onto the final ridge, passing the signed Mt. Walter (13,141 feet). It can be extremely windy along the ridge. Continue another 0.25 of a mile to Wheeler Peak, making sure to head straight when the trail forks to the left.

Congratulations, you're standing on the highest point in New Mexico

(Waypoint 2). The views are fantastic from here. The summit register is inside the pipe (see Photo 4). It can be difficult to remove the lid. Enjoy the views!

PHOTO 4

To Descend: Retrace your steps.

WAYPOINTS:
1. 36.59708N / 105.44908W
2. 36.55688N / 105.41698W

Glossary

bouldering: Using hands and feet to climb over, around, or down large boulders. Most bouldering routes are in the canyons of Red Rock.

buttress: A large flat portion of rock that stands out from a wall behind it.

cairn: A pile of rocks used to mark a path or route.

canyon: A deep narrow valley with high steep sides.

catch basin: A depression in sandstone where water collects.

chimney: A steep narrow chute with parallel walls.

chute: A steep well-worn passage. A chute is larger than a crack, but smaller than a gully.

closed loop: A trail or path that makes a complete circle.

conglomerate: A rock composed of many types of pebbles and minerals.

crack: A fracture in a rock; varies in size.

crag: A sandstone wall scaled by technical climbers.

cryptobiotic soil: A fragile type of soil found near Lake Mead. Do not walk on it.

face: The steep side of a mountain.

fall: A normally dry place that becomes a waterfall when it rains or snows. A dry fall is a class 2 or higher climb.

gully: A broad low-angled depression that runs vertically down the side of a mountain.

narrows: A tight passageway in a wash, formed by wind and water erosion over thousands of years.

open loop: A trail or path that makes an incomplete circle. The trailhead and the trail's end are in different locations.

pass: An obvious cleft or break in a ridgeline where it's possible to cross.

path: A non-maintained pathway that's more difficult to follow than a trail, but easier to follow than a route. Some paths are former trails that have become overgrown or faded.

pullout: A place to park along a paved road. A pullout is either paved or made of gravel or dirt.

ramp: An inclined sandstone ledge.

ravine: A small, narrow, steep-sided valley that's larger than a gully, but smaller than a canyon.

rock scrambling: Class 2 and class 3 climbing up and over rock without the use of ropes.

route: A trek that's hiked by using landmarks. There are no marked paths or trails to follow.

saddle: A low point between two peaks, ridgelines, or high points.

sandstone: Porous rock made of sand.

scree: An accumulation of small rocks found on a slope.

slope: A very low-angled face of a mountain.

summit: The peak of a mountain.

switchback: The zigzag pattern in a trail or path that makes it easier to go up the side of a mountain.

talus: Loose rock and gravel on a slope.

tank: A place larger than a catch basin where water gathers after a rainstorm.

topo map: A map showing the details of the contour of the land by means of lines and symbols.

trail: A well-maintained pathway that's easy to follow.

trailhead: The starting point of a trail, path, or route.

vista: A distant view from a high point or peak.

About the Author

Branch Whitney, also the author of *Hiking Southern Nevada*, *Hiking Las Vegas*, and *Hiking the High Sierra*, has led more than 2,000 hikers to more than 100 different summits in southern Nevada and beyond. He has named over 25 peaks in southern Nevada and has found over 60 routes. His website (hikinglasvegas.com) is the primary source for hiking and mountaineering information for southern Nevada.

About Huntington Press

Huntington Press is a specialty publisher of Las Vegas- and gambling-related books and periodicals, including the award-winning consumer newsletter, *Anthony Curtis' Las Vegas Advisor*.

Huntington Press
3665 Procyon Street
Las Vegas, Nevada 89103

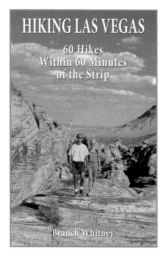
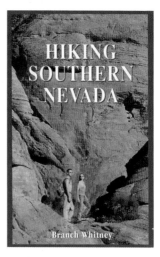